Spouses of Sex Addicts

Hope for The Journey

Formerly S.A.R.A.H. (Spouses of Addicts
Rebuilding and Healing)

Richard Blankenship

Spouses of Sex Addicts
Hope for The Journey
by Richard Blankenship

Printed in the United States of America

ISBN 9781609576356

Cover design by BMC Graphics of Norcross, Georgia.

www.xulonpress.com

Table of Contents

What others are saying about
S.A.R.A.H.
(endorsements of the first edition)

"**L**ike Sarah of old, this book encourages wives of addicts to take on a new name and to move beyond hopeless skepticism and pain into God's healing blessings. The writers of S.A.R.A.H. impart such a practical, compassionate wisdom based on years of experience. A must read for spouses who wants to embark on a hope-filled journey of rebuilding their lives beyond the ravages of sexual addiction."

Doug Rosenau, Ed.D., author of *A Celebration of Sex; Soul Virgins*.

"This book will be an encouragement and source of valuable information for spouses who are reeling from the reality of sexual addiction in their partners. I'm grateful that this book is there to provide healthy, appropriate information mixed with real life stories that impart wisdom and hope; not hope in what the addict chooses to do or not do, but hope in the ability of the spouse to recover and grow in spite of the devastation of sexual addiction."

Dr. Barbara Steffens, Steffens Counseling Services, Adjunct Professor – Indiana Wesleyan University, University of Phoenix, Co-author of *Your Sexually Addicted Spouse*

"Few people have as much experience working with Sexual Addiction and its effects on families as Richard Blankenship. It is my prayer that the concepts and stories he presents in SARAH will be encouraging, comforting and offer direction to those spouses beginning their journey of recovery."

Debra Taylor, Certified Sex Therapist, co-author of *Secrets of Eve: Understanding the Mystery of Female Sexuality,*

"Richard's book provides wonderful insights and truths regarding sexual addiction. I'm grateful that he asked me to share in this project. You will discover practical examples that are honestly spoken. Knowledge is indeed powerful. His pages are replete with truth, empathy, viable solutions, and encouragement for your personal road of recovery. Make sure to have a highlighter pen with you as you study this book. You will return many times to revisit the insights that God will bring to you concerning the changes He desires to make in your life. Through his writings, you will be challenged to find the child of God who is indeed free, whole and living in grace. God's blessings to you!"

Debbie Whitcomb – grateful recovering spouse of a sex addict

"Richard and this amazing group of contributors have faithfully pursued the vision that is S.A.R.A.H. with diligence and passion, and the result is a significant source of hope and wisdom to the spouses of sexual addicts. They have known or seen the pain and grief, either personally or as a counselor; and they willingly share from their hearts in order to help others navigate the physical, emotional, mental and spiritual obstacles in the journey to recovery. It's a journey of personal transformation that must take place if the spouse is to survive and beyond that to thrive. As Richard says in the concluding pages, there are "Pearls of Wisdom" here; pearls of great value to suffering spouses and to those who counsel and guide them on the journey."

Bob Hale, President and Co-founder
L.I.F.E. Ministries International

S.A.R.A.H. is the most helpful thing I have read. I came to a spouses group desperate to find help. I left with a renewed hope and desire to live in a more healthy way. It's now been three years since I started this journey. This is a book that is written from the voice of experience. It builds a vision of hope. My prayer is that every reader can experience the hope and healing that God has in store for your life.

Amanda R., - grateful recovery spouse of a sex addict

This book is about a difficult, isolating, and unique situation that thousands of spouses find themselves thrown into with feelings of hopelessness and emotional pain. Planting seeds of possible solutions and choices, Mr. Blankenship relates the processes these individuals and couples may experience with the promise of a future that is better than their today.

Sharon Borntrager, MA, CPSAS
National Coalition for the Protection of Children & Families

My Knight

My knight sat stately upon his steed
Bedecked in his full armor
Sword raised high and aim precise
To defend my love and honor

My gaze told all that was in my heart
Undying love, respect and devotion
My knight embodied all my soul
My hopes, my dreams and emotion

Then the mighty cry was given
The battle did ensue
Knight to knight, sword to sword
So easy to subdue

Reeling from his fatal wound
My knight fell hard and fast
Deception falling from my eyes
I saw the truth at last

He had no chance in battle
All was lost before the start
He was really unprotected
No armor on his heart

All my dreams and plans
Now 'round me shattered
Shards of hope embodied in a man
Now in the dust are scattered

My handsome knight before this day
I never knew his flaw
But my Lord and King, before I was
All my days he saw

He scooped me up
And held me tight
Kissed my heart and made it right

With tender love
My heart in hand
He showed me how
I had worshipped a man

-Faithful and True Atlanta Spouse

"This is my heart. Some hope, but tattered, torn, and bandages from all of the wounds."
Made during a Faithful and True Marriages spouses workshop

Introduction

B eing the spouse of a sex addict has gotten you into a sorority
you never wanted to join. Yet, you find yourself in the middle
of navigating a rushing river. Not only do you feel up the river
without a paddle, you also wouldn't have ever thought you needed
one. The raging river on the cover of this book is somewhat like the
journey of a spouse.[1] Upon discovering that you are married to a
sexual addict, you are set adrift on a raging stream. It feels like your
existence is threatened. The currents are heavy and the undertow is
strong, threatening to drown you at any second. The boulders, rocks,
and branches strike you inflicting more pain as you float through
dangerous waters. Learning to navigate a boat in strong currents
becomes overwhelming.

Spouses of Sex Addicts is about navigating those waters.
S.A.R.A.H. is an acrostic (Spouses of Addicts Rebuilding and
Healing,) but the name also holds significance by discussing the
real people who owned it, especially the very first "Sarah". When
Abraham was called by God to take his new name, Sarah was also
called to take hers as she faced new challenges and opportunities.
All of those who have been called out of addiction have had to learn
their new names, but this is just as important for the spouses to take
their new names and learn how to live out a fresh, rebuilt life. The
journey truly has its rough waters.

Spouses typically don't try to help their husband's act out. In
Abraham's sexual acting out, Sarah was an accomplice, because it

---

[1] The original SARAH cover had a river with boulders that were a metaphor for
the journey of healing.

was she who brought her servant to sleep with Abraham to provide children. Most spouses are not purposely helping their mates act out. *Spouses of Sex Addicts* is about realizing how we sometimes unknowingly enable our spouses and learning how we need to change as well. The old solutions won't work anymore.

Sarah laughed when the strangers said she was to have children, because she was convinced that she was too old for her life to be fruitful and have such wonderful blessing. Part of overcoming the trauma of betrayal is the mourning of time and dreams that were lost, and, though at certain points it seems too much to believe, to have faith and hope that the future will be positive. *Spouses of Sex Addicts* is about being patient with God's redemption, and how sometimes the healing comes to us when we think it is past possible. It feels like the only thing that can be done is to survive, but it is about more than just surviving, it's about rebuilding and thriving. The discovery of your partner's sexual acting out is one of the most devastating realizations you will ever experience. However, rough waters that seem impossibly difficult can be mastered with help.

There are some boulders in the water that can't be moved and must be accepted. Obstacles can appear from any direction at any time. They can force you to change direction and to make adjustments that you might not want to make. Sometimes it's necessary to survive the changing current. The timing and route you take may change along the way. The end won't look like you expect, but it will probably be better and sweeter.

Like the original Sarah, the journey of a spouse can be described as an emotional roller coaster. Some days it will seem as if you are fighting with everything you have to climb to the top of the hill. The depression, frustration, and self-doubt can drain you of your energy. At times, it is like you coast along for awhile but then encounter sharp turns. There are dips along the way that will create fear and anxiety. Then there are the large drops into the land of uncertainty. Feeling out of control and that you are in constant danger will be common. The landings aren't smooth. The journey is unpredictable.

Navigating the journey of a spouse has physical, emotional, mental, and spiritual obstacles to deal with. Many well-meaning but misinformed people may enter your life along the way. Spouses are often blamed for their partner's acting out. They are told to be more sexual, never say no, dress differently, have plastic surgery, and cook better meals. Some myths tell spouses that if they don't have sex with their partner every three days that their husbands will probably act out. When you have been betrayed and wounded, the last thing on your mind is having sex with the person who has wounded you. Some writers, even Christian writers, say things that are medically wrong. Another fiction tells wives if their husbands don't ejaculate every 72 hours that they will "explode." Spouses may hear concepts like this from church leaders, friends, and others. This type of advice creates more problems than it solves. For this reason, we emphasize concepts of spiritual abuse throughout this book.

Spouses have been made to feel responsible for solving their partner's addiction problems. I have worked with people who have come out of abusive religious practices for years. There have even been religious groups with rules that wives had to have sex with their husbands at least 4 times per week. The reason that they gave for this practice was so that their husbands "wouldn't be tempted to lust." The fundamental problem with this concept is that it makes the wife responsible for her husband's purity and completely distorts the intimate mutual lovemaking that is encouraged in I Corinthians 7:1-6. He is then free to blame her, be selfish and accept no personal responsibility for his own sexuality. In the same way, spouses who are told that they must be sexual with their partners are made to feel responsible for helping control an addiction when in reality, they are powerless. The addict is responsible for sexual choices, not the spouse.

There is no greater honor in the world than to be allowed to share in someone else's pain.

The journey begins with a difficult period of grieving. Coping with loss is a major theme throughout this book. Understanding your family of origin, trauma, and wounds are critical in your journey. Coping with issues of spirituality, religion, and the role of the church are addressed. We look at practical issues of managing emotions, healing in community, disclosure, and myths that you may encounter. We are grateful to the spouses who were willing to share their stories in this book. Their names and other identifying information have been changed to protect their anonymity. These are all spouses that Heath, Joyce, Debbie and I have worked with over the years. We asked people who are at different places in the journey to share their stories. Almost 150 responded with a desire to help others. You will read the stories of people who are new in recovery and those who have years of experience.

The complex part of the journey is in identifying what your issues are. This book will help you look at what you bring to the dance. We all bring baggage into marriage. The bags need to be unpacked. *Spouses of Sex Addicts* is about *you* and it is for *you*. It is not about the addict in your life. Along the way, you will meet people and experience friendships and intimate relationships in ways you've never dreamed. Recovery will change your theology. Your relationship with God will never be the same. It can grow beyond your wildest dreams.

Marriages can not only survive, they can thrive. Realistically, we can't guarantee that your marriage will make it. This book is about hope. My friend Debbie Laaser has had tremendous influence on me through her work with spouses. She writes of her marriage to Mark. Debbie says that after recovery, the marriage was beyond what she would have ever imagined.[1]

Spouses groups are my personal favorites. When I began forming Faithful and True – Atlanta, there were no spouses groups being conducted by therapists in the Atlanta area. We immediately began having spouses who would drive to our center from 4 different states because they couldn't find people who specialized in working with spouses and sex addicts. A major focus from the beginning was to form the best outreach to spouses we possibly could. God has blessed us with hundreds of spouses to work with over the years. My coworker, Joyce Tomblin, and I write of some of our experiences in the chapter on myths of the journey. People who are in relationships with sex addicts or those with sexual integrity issues (both men and women) are very near and dear to our hearts at Faithful and True Atlanta.

The impact of sexual addiction on children must not be overlooked. Spouse's groups have occasionally included parents of sex addicts. Children are learning how to be married from their parents. Appendix C addresses these issues.

There is no greater honor in the world than to be allowed to share in someone else's pain. I'm grateful to all of the spouses that have given me the privilege of walking with them through their journey of healing. These ladies and men have transformed me, my marriage and family, and my work, more than any one group of people.

Nothing unites a group of people more than sharing their stories and their pain. Spouses groups bond quickly for this reason. When a new group or intensive workshop begins, there is a sense of heaviness in the air as we begin dealing with the overwhelming feelings of grief and loss. As we share and grow together, these feelings are eventually replaced with hope, purpose, and a sense of direction. It isn't a quick fix. It's a journey of transformation.

Spouses of Sex Addicts is about that courageous journey, as it was for the Biblical Sarah. It is the taking of a new name and stepping out in faith. This expedition becomes how your new name will be owned as you bravely live out the rebuilding and healing process. Embark on this journey just for you as a spouse. It's not about the addict in your life. Life may feel unmanageable if you are trying to manage things (your mate's journey) you can't ultimately do anything about. Again, this book is about you and it's for you. Reading this book may be one of the first steps you've taken on your trip towards greater wholeness. There are resources in the back to guide you towards further sources of help. Thank you for allowing us into your life as we share together in a journey of healing.

A Word About Labels

One of the struggles our team of writers had in creating S.A.R.A.H. was in the use of labels. I (Richard) made the decision that the words "co-addict" and "codependent" wouldn't be used. I believe I used the word "codependent" one time and it was in relationship to my own story. In our groups and workshops for partners of sex addicts, we struggle with what to call them. The term "spouse's group" implies that it is only for those married to sex addicts. In years past, we have included people who were dating sex addicts, parents of addicts, and those who have been previously married to a sex addict. The labels are unfortunately a necessary evil.

The term "codependent" has been used excessively to the point its meaning has been diluted. A common assumption is that all spouses of sex addicts are codependent. *The stereotype isn't true.* Not all spouses exhibit codependent traits. Some spouses do benefit from addressing issues of codependency. We must be careful about over generalizing this term. Improper labeling can discourage people from getting the necessary help in recovery.

The term "co-addict" is controversial. Early on, I used this term very loosely. Years ago when I began specializing in working with families of sex addicts, I was taught that this term meant "anyone who is in a relationship with a sex addict." The latter meant a person could be born a co-addict if one of their parents was an alcoholic or drug addict. Being a close friend or family member of an addict would get you the label "co-addict." Spouses were labeled as "relationship addicts" when they chose to stay married to a sex addict. *Over the years, I've learned that the stereotypes simply aren't true.*

The term "co-addict" has its roots in the 12-step movement of Alcoholics Anonymous. In studying its background, I've since learned the implications of this deep-rooted term are not appropriate for many spouses of sex addicts. Don't let the misuse of labels prevent you from getting the help you need.

Spouses of sex addicts are trauma survivors. Dr. Barbara Steffens[2] conducted the best research to date on the impact of disclosure on spouses of sex addicts. Much of the chaos and "acting out" of a spouse (a term clearly rooted in 12-step theory) is a result of trauma, not relationship addiction. Grief and trauma will make people do things that they wouldn't do otherwise as they desperately seek to restore safety and stability to their lives.

The 12-step movement has saved the lives of millions of people across the world. I love the results and have seen many sex addicts and spouses benefit from working the steps. There is much wisdom in many of the 12-step slogans and material. As I reflected on my roots in this field, I notice that those who have insisted on a "coaddiction" model instead of a trauma model were recovering sex addicts. In some cases they were working out their own issues on spouses. All had benefited from 12-step models but were unintentionally inflicting harm on spouses.

Labels are a necessary evil. We use them to communicate. Because of the far reaching implications, it is important care be taken in their use. Don't worry about labeling yourself as you read this book. Just absorb what you need in order to move forward in your journey of healing and transformation.

Chapter One

I Can't Believe This Is Happening . . .

"I'll never forget that day. I went to the computer to get directions to the place where my son would be playing his first ball game. I had no idea that my life was about to be changed forever in this simple little act. As soon as I typed in the name of the park, the images of sexual acts I never thought I would see suddenly imprinted themselves onto my brain. With two clicks of a mouse, I had just discovered my husband's secret. I had been replaced with Internet pornography."

-Carrie

"I was sick to my stomach. I logged onto the computer to get a recipe and there it was – my husband's cesspool. I sat in shock as the pornographic images came popping up faster than I could stop them. I called my husband and told him to meet me at Richard's office. He confessed when I confronted him. I had to leave in the middle of the session to throw up. I was overwhelmed and had no idea what to do. It was like an out of body experience – this couldn't be happening to me."

-Maureen

"It started for me the afternoon that the phone bill came. There were numbers I didn't recognize. I was calling to check to see if it was an error on the bill. She answered the phone. It wasn't long before I discovered that she was my husband's affair partner. I was devastated. He denied it over and over, but finally came clean. I didn't eat or sleep for three days. I kept asking myself "what does she have that I don't?" At times, I still can't believe I have lived to tell about it. A part of me died that day."

-Emily

"The credit card bill came in the mail and I didn't know what to think. I normally don't pay the bills, but something told me to look that day. I saw all of these entries for an interior decorator. I knew we hadn't used any services like that so I called the phone number. It was an escort service. Words can't describe the level of anger I felt as I began to realize that my world was being turned upside down. My husband had a trophy collection. I shattered every one of them. In my anger I destroyed my wedding ring. It meant nothing to him so why should I keep wearing it? I had kept our marriage vows. Why couldn't he?"

-Tonya

"I don't know how I will ever be able to trust a man again. He has deceived me, cheated on me, used pornography, potentially exposed our children to his Internet history, and I feel treated like garbage. I'm hurt, angry, scared half to death – how will I survive this? I can't sleep and my stomach feels like it's tied in knots. My head hurts so bad it feels like I've been run over by an eighteen wheeler. Oh God this hurts. I don't want to be divorced but I don't think I can stand to be with him another minute. I don't know what to do."

-Marion

"She finally told me what I had feared all along. She was seeing another man. She flaunted it in my face at first. The shame was incredible. I felt like I wasn't good enough. What would people think if they found out? I just tried to keep her from telling anyone. I tried to control her and got more frustrated. During that first month I thought I was going to die. I woke up some mornings mad that God had let me live through the night."

-Don

Overwhelming grief. As I read the words shared generously from the journals of spouses of sex addicts, these two words keep coming to mind. Names have been changed to preserve confidentiality. These are the entries made in journals during the first days following the discovery that they were married to a sex addict.

If you are in relationship with someone with sexual integrity issues, this book is for you. You may be a spouse, parent, child, or close friend who has been affected by someone's sexual acting out. What is the journey like? What can I do to heal? How will I survive? Is it possible to get through this? What will it take?

The stories above reveal an experience of grief that appears to defy reality. One spouse shared with me that the discovery of her husband's sexual addiction was almost as bad as when she lost a child in a car accident. Others have likened the grief to losing a child at birth or a miscarriage.

The discovery of his/her sex addiction brings with it great loss. The loss of trust, dreams, and hope will feel like someone has plunged a knife into the deepest part of your heart. You didn't believe you would face anything like this when you walked down the aisle on your wedding day and took vows before God to remain faithful. How could this happen to you?

Much has been written about the grief cycle. Elizabeth Kubler Ross was a pioneer in this process in her landmark book, "On Death and Dying." I've chosen not to make this a clinical lesson on the grief cycle. Instead the words of experience will communicate the concepts of shock, anger, depression, and other parts of grief in ways that no clinician can describe.

The journey of a spouse begins with grief. This is where healing begins. Without a time of grief, healing will be delayed and the devastation will continue. We scream the word "WHY" in our pain. We shake uncontrollably, experience panic attacks, and get physically sick.

In his book "Experiencing Grief," Norm Wright shares these words from a grieving father.

"Grief is like a wave. It comes rolling in from a far-off place. I could no more push it back than if I were standing in the water at the beach. I could not fight the wave. It moved over me and under me

and broke against me, but I could never stop it. It yielded to my pres-
ence and in so yielding arrived at its destination. It worked around
me. The harder I fought it, the more exhausted I became. So it is with
grief. If I tried to fight it, it would vanquish me. If I pushed it down
it would stick in my soul and emerge as something else: depression,
bitterness, exhaustion. If I yielded to the waves and let it carry me,
however, it would take me to a new place."

With grief, the harder we try to avoid it, the heavier the burden
becomes. The losses aren't clean. It's like someone came along and
ripped a part of your identity from your heart. Reality has gone, marriage as you have known it has gone, innocence has been tossed to
the wind, confidence has been shattered, a sense of loss of femininity
(or masculinity for male spouses) eats at your identity. Friends, in-
laws, and other relationships will disappear or change, and life feels
hopeless. There may be the loss of a best friend, sexual relationship,
and a support system that you and your spouse had developed as a
couple that will need to be grieved. Coming face to face with raw
emotions will feel like surgery being conducted without anesthesia.

Grief can feel like you are in a wrestling match with God.

I remember well the day I came face to face with the reality of
loss in my life. The feelings were indescribable, especially since I
didn't have an emotional vocabulary. I share more of this journey of
grief, depression, and trauma in chapter 3. Part of living in a fallen
world involves grieving losses. The Psalms are full of examples.

Melissa Haas has a ministry to hurting spouses. She has shaped
much of my thinking on the grieving process for spouses of sexual
addicts. Melissa has graciously written her story for this book. She
writes as a sister in the journey and as someone who has intimately
experienced the grief that comes with being married to a sex addict.
Most of this chapter is Melissa's work. She has also written the
"L.I.F.E. Guide for Spouses" which includes exercises for helping
you through the grieving process. Her work has reshaped my
thinking about the journey of a spouse. She is authentic, and speaks
from many years of experience. As you read Melissa's story, notice

her grief and how it turns into hope. Someone once said "the only way through it is through it." This isn't the most hopeful sounding statement. Melissa shows us how there is hope and healing that can come in the wake of devastating grief and loss.

Melissa's story

"It is for freedom that Christ has set us free," Galatians 5:1 says. Ten years ago, if you would have asked me if I was free, I would have looked at you with confusion in my eyes and replied, "Well, yes. Of course, I'm free." You see, I knew in my mind that I was free because of Christ's death for me on the cross. Intellectually, I understood that, in Christ, sin no longer held me captive, that I was no longer bound to live out the curse sin brought on me through Adam and Eve. But, my life didn't feel very free. In fact, trapped would have been a better word to describe how I felt.

Looking back, I know the trap was laid for me when I was girl and hungry for my father's love and approval. I longed to be desired by a man—spiritually, emotionally, and sexually. And so, when I met Troy, I knew my dreams had come true. Saved out of a lifestyle of drug addiction and sexual promiscuity, Troy was on-fire for God and passionate about helping broken people find Christ. And he desired me, wanted me, was infatuated with me. While I was passionately embracing this lover of my soul and body, I couldn't see the trap closing around me. All I could see was that this man loved me and wanted to spend the rest of his life with me.

Our relationship was unhealthy and sinful from the very start. I was so needy, desperate, really for a man's affection. Troy thought I was his savior—a good, godly girl who would help him forget the shame of his past life and help him realize all of his dreams. It wasn't very long until the relationship became sexual—even though I had promised myself and God that I would not give myself away before marriage. We felt guilty but powerless to stop. And we both rationalized that we were engaged and so, it was like we were married anyway. Besides, we felt called to the mission field. We had great plans and a wonderful calling from God. And God in His mercy, allowed us to go.

We were appointed as the youngest career missionary couple ever assigned to the field by the International Mission Board in June of 1993. I was 24, and Troy was 26. Married then for two years, the world and all of our dreams of missionary service were before us. We chose an assignment in Kenya, and landed in Nairobi in late 1993. Neither one of us was aware of how unhealthy and immature we really were.

Once on the mission field, our marriage began to deteriorate rapidly. Troy's anger became more of a problem than it had ever been before. I felt more and more unloved. But, we were doing great work as missionaries. I blamed it on culture shock and prayed for God to work in his heart. I made excuses for him and tried to hide the effects of his anger on me when we were with other people. But, I couldn't help wondering if there was something more. Our sexual relationship became non-existent. After I got pregnant with our first child, we didn't have sex for over a year. I was devastated by the rejection of my husband. It had come full circle for me. I had married him because I felt so desired by him. And now, he had completely rejected me physically, as well as spiritually and emotionally. I felt like a maid, a secretary, a co-worker, a servant—but not anything like a wife.

By 1997, our marriage was so painful, I had begun to pray for God to either kill Troy or kill me. To cope with the pain of his rejection, I turned to romance novels, romantic movies, fantasy, and masturbation. Whenever I had a spare moment from our missionary work, I lived in a magical fantasy world where my husband loved me and did wonderful, romantic things for me.

Troy was just as miserable as I was—only I couldn't understand why. At first I thought it was all me, that I was somehow failing him. But after trying everything to change, to please, to placate, I began to realize that I wasn't doing anything to deserve the anger and criticism and abuse I constantly received. Something was wrong in Troy's heart. Looking back, I see now all of the signs I missed and overlooked.

It was easy to overlook them all, though. We both poured ourselves into ministry to hide our pain, to balance the bad in our marriage. We lived and worked with an unreached people group in northern Kenya, and God was doing wonderful and miraculous things among them. The IMB sent their journalists to write a story about our work. We were even featured in the 1998 international missions study. Troy spoke at the pastor's conference of the SBC in June of 1999, and as a result of all the exposure, several people joined our team to minister to the Turkana people.

On this side of that time in our lives, I see now that God was putting into place a team of people who would continue to minister to the people of Turkana in our absence. For it was time to dismantle the great façade Troy and I had built during our six and a half years on the mission field. And when His time was right, God did just that. I call it the merciful unveiling in our lives. In November of 1999, two of the women Troy had been involved with sexually came forward to confess what was happening. It was the beginning of the end of our missionary career.

At the time I was 39 weeks pregnant and unable to travel by plane. Troy was sent immediately back to the States to a counseling center. I stayed behind with our three-year old daughter to have the baby, pack up, and say good-bye. It was very painful. I remember, though, the first night I sat alone in the guest house. Part of my heart knew that this was the answer I had been looking for. But part of me couldn't begin to comprehend that my husband had been unfaithful and that all that we had was lost. As I sat there—numb and in shock—I remember feeling a great warmth like a soft, fleecy blanket wrapped around me. And the Lord said, "Melissa, I am answering your prayers." It was a message that helped me get through the next weeks and months.

Three weeks later, I landed in the States with our newborn son and daughter. We joined Troy at the counseling center where God began putting our lives and our marriage back together again. There was more painful information for me to learn—what had been disclosed in Kenya was only the tip of the iceberg. There were tremendous losses to grieve. There were family and friends and supporters to tell. Life was upside down. And yet, little by little, God restored our hope that He was able to free us from the life we had been living—Troy bound up in sexual addiction, me bound up in my need for Troy's love and my sinful ways of coping with his rejection.

It's been six years now since God took out his scalpel and cut open our infected hearts. I've learned so much about my Father. I've come to know Him more intimately than I ever thought possible. I've taken Troy and Troy's love for me off the throne of my heart, and put God back in His rightful place. I've begun to enjoy, for the first time in my life, the freeing power of authentic relationships. I've taken to heart all of the "one another's" in the Bible, and not perfectly, but consistently, I now walk in freedom.

God's restoration process in Troy's life and in our marriage has been nothing short of amazing. Troy has become a man of integrity and grace. And, as God would have it, we now minister together again. Not as international missionaries this time, but as two broken people walking with other broken people on the journey of transformation and freedom. I can honestly say that I would not trade the pain of the journey. For it is in my suffering and His sufficient grace through it that I have found freedom—freedom not just in my head, but in my heart.

What are you feeling as you read these words? Shock, anger, rage, hurt, pain, sadness, despair, hope, joy, and compassion are just a few of the things you might have felt. My guess is that you have experienced a variety of feelings. It's ok. You feel what you feel. As you grieve, your feelings will change and you will experience high's and low's. It's like riding a roller coaster without a railing and it feels like the cars will jump the track at any moment. For me, grief and depression feel helpless. It's like you are going down a greased slide into disaster, and you are helpless to do anything to stop it. For grief to heal, it must be experienced. Consider some more of Melissa's powerful words as you begin your journey.

"I look back at that time in my life and wonder how in the world I survived. Troy's betrayal was worse than a death in many ways. I kept looking at this man I thought I knew and wondering how I could have been so wrong about him, and why the God I trusted had let me marry him. I was angry, I was sad, I was numb, and I was confused. Some days I felt hopeful and at peace. And then there were the dark days when despair hung over my head like a black cloud. Of course, there were also the angry days when just seeing Troy triggered overwhelming feelings of rage. I felt so out of control. One minute I would be fine, and the next minute tears would be running down my face. I wasn't going crazy, though. I was simply grieving."[3]

Can you relate to these words? Have you run the gamut of emotions? The good news is you aren't going crazy. You aren't losing your mind and you will heal. This is what it's like to experience the grief that comes with discovering your partner's sexual addiction.

A common question is, "how long will it last?" The bad news is that there is no timetable. Feelings of grief can be triggered over time. The grief process isn't linear. You will go in and out of various emotions and stages. Grief is like having an infection cut out of your heart. The process hurts deeply at first, but it's the beginning of a healing journey that will strengthen your heart and life.

Finding safe people to share your grief with can speed up the process. We are created to be in relationship. As I have struggled with personal grief over the last year, the most devastating loss I experienced was the loss of friendships. Grieving any loss in isolation is more difficult than healing in community. Finding that safe environment is difficult, especially since part of the issues that spouses experience involve finding unhealthy relationships. Failing to grow and heal will lead you into more unhealthy relationships.[4]

One of the most difficult struggles for Christian spouses is coping with anger. Dysfunctional beliefs about anger will be addressed in the chapter on spiritual abuse. It's important to remember that anger is a God-given emotion. Denying your anger will prolong the grieving process. You have been betrayed and wounded deeply by someone who has made a commitment to be a safe person in your life. Anger is appropriate. It can be expressed in ways that are appropriate. It's also important to remember that anger is a secondary emotion, usually preceded by fear. Give appropriate voice to your anger. Also, give voice to your fears. There are fears of rejection, powerlessness, hopelessness, abandonment, failure, inadequacy, isolation, loneliness, and relationships.[5]

I don't like pain. I don't handle it well. I have a very low tolerance for physical pain. Emotional pain can be more devastating.

Coming to grips with the pain of the journey is extremely hard, but necessary. You will take this journey at your own pace. Don't let anyone tell you that you should be where they think you should be. Grief is managed in bite-sized chunks. Some days you may feel like you can eat the whole monster, other days you will be on a liquid only diet. Take care of yourself during this journey. Let yourself grieve at your own pace.

"The truth is when we put a time limit on the grieving process, we are trying to manage and control our pain. Unfortunately we are also preventing the healing God wants to bring in our lives."

Grief can feel like you are in a wrestling match with God. It feels like you are pinned to the mat and that you can't get back on your feet. The Old Testament is full of stories of people who agonized through long journeys of grief as they faced the loss of relationships, land, possessions, promises, hopes, and dreams. When the pain gets to be more than we can bear, it is tempting to seek false solutions and try to escape the journey of grief. You will wrestle with the loss of your faith. This is a journey that will change your relationship with God. At times it will feel like faith is worthless. At other times, it may feel like the only thing you have to hang onto. You may question the very existence of God. You are in good company. Many great men and women throughout the Bible had doubts, and their faith was strengthened anyway.

C.S. Lewis writes of his journey of grief and healing. He refers to the "mad midnight moments" in which you question everything you have ever believed about God, marriage, life, and death.[6] Grief will be worse at different times. One pattern I've seen in Christians is that Saturday evening is a difficult time. Perhaps it was when you and your husband would be preparing for Sunday school and worship activities. And now there is an empty space to fill. Night time may be when you are vulnerable. When you are physically tired you will be emotionally tired. I think of the many nights of wrestling in bed, fighting the feelings and fears, and desperately wanting to go to sleep and not wake up. Depression and grief will make you question whether life is worth living.

Grief may have a different face for you than the person sitting next to you. It's a journey that doesn't have a clear ending point.

Part of what determines how we go through the grieving process relates to how we've been trained to grieve throughout life. If you have been allowed to grieve losses and acknowledge feelings during childhood losses, you are more likely to allow yourself to grieve in a normal, healthy way. I hear the heartbreaking stories of people who weren't allowed to cry at the death of a family member during their childhood. This trains people to stuff feelings and not grieve normally when they are faced with crisis and loss.

Another factor that determines the intensity of grief is the level of invasiveness involved in the loss. If your car is broken into while you are away and the cd player is stolen, you will be disappointed and upset as you face your loss. If the same cd player is stolen by someone who puts a gun in your face and threatens your life, the level of grieving is more intense. Recuperating from a cut on your arm is one thing. Having a limb amputated involves more devastating effects and will require a longer period of grief. The pain of betrayal is like losing a limb. You have a long period of healing ahead of you.

Regardless of how you have been taught to grieve by your family of origin and other life experiences, the onset of sudden trauma brings the most difficult type of grief you can experience. The discovery of your spouse's sexual addiction is one of the most traumatic events you will face throughout life. Some losses allow people time to prepare. A friend or relative who is dying from an illness may be a longer process, but it gives people time to begin grieving and accept the truth. The fall of 1997 was a time of grief and loss for me. During that time my family buried two of my grandparents. When my grandmother died in September, I wasn't expecting this to happen. She had been very healthy throughout her 89 years and looked great when I last saw her three weeks before she died. Her death wasn't one that I had much time to prepare for. Seven weeks later my grandfather passed away. He had deteriorated gradually and his death didn't surprise us. In fact, he had prepared for his own funeral service many years before. The fact that my grief was different didn't mean that I loved one grandparent more than another. One loss involved a long period of time while the other was more of a surprise.

One client I worked with had a husband who was in the world trade center on 9/11. They had come to therapy early in 2001 as they struggled with grieving the loss of Jenny's parents. Jenny and Martin did well as they went through their grief. It was a loss they had anticipated. On September 11 another type of grief entered their lives. The U.S. was attacked by terrorists. Martin was in the world trade center when the first plane hit. He didn't survive. Jenny struggled at first with why this loss was so different. Several thousand people experienced what I call "shock" grief that day. There was no time to prepare for the loss resulting from a surprise attack. Spouses of sex addicts experience shock grief upon discovery of the pornography, affair partner, or whatever form the addiction takes.

"Grieving well involves accepting the pain of the journey - not denying it, nor running away from it, and not trying to fix it. No one who is emotionally and spiritually healthy enjoys pain. Even our Lord prayed intensely that He would not have to endure the cross set before Him. Only God can give us the grace to say, "It's a journey filled with excruciating pain, but I choose your will over mine. I choose the journey you have laid out for me, Father, instead of my plans and my agenda."[7]

What are some practical guidelines for grieving? What will the grieving process be like when traveling the road of the healing journey? Melissa gives a snapshot of the journey.

- You admit to yourself how bad it really is.
- You feel pain and anger and are able to talk about your feelings with safe people.
- You refrain from trusting your spouse too soon.
- You allow yourself to grieve.
- You seek out trustworthy women/men with whom you can share your soul.
- You begin to recognize that the only one you can be responsible for is you.
- You begin to set healthy limits in your marriage and other relationships.
- You give yourself to God everyday.

- You are able to see God's faithfulness through the losses and you reach out to Him for strength and comfort.[8]

Overwhelming Emotions: Coping With Crisis

"I'm having feelings I have never experienced before. Some days it feels like I'm going to crack up. The thought of what he did with those pictures makes me sick. And then I feel guilty about feeling so angry, like I should be able to get over it. I feel violated and mistreated. The pain feels unbearable."

Margaret

"Suffering is a place where clichés don't work and words often fail. I was at lunch last week with a friend who is in the middle of some difficult days and I don't have any answers. I just don't. I can't fix it for him. I've tried. And we sat there and talked and ate, and I let him know that I'm in it with him. It isn't very pretty and it isn't very fun, but when we join each other in the pain and confusion, God is there. Sometimes it means we sit in silence for awhile, not knowing what to say. And find out that with these people around us, we can make it through anything. And that gives us something to celebrate."[9]

How do you cope with overwhelming emotions? The grieving described in the previous chapter will take you on an emotional roller coaster. Look at some of the feeling words in appendix A. Words under the categories of *depression, sadness, anxiety, fear, distress, inadequate, guilt, fear, shame,* and *anger* will describe the emotions that spouses experience during the crisis of betrayal.

In the early days of this journey, you will feel beaten down, tired, and emotionally drained. It's not unusual to experience symptoms of physical illness (headaches, nausea, and vomiting) during a time of crisis. I am used to seeing spouses have to leave my office to vomit. The shock of realizing you are married to someone with sexual integrity issues will make you feel out of control. Tears will flow uncontrollably and you will wonder if it's possible to ever feel good again. You may feel so devastated that you consider suicide. You may feel like you want God to take you home. The entire world will feel chaotic. And you will feel like a prisoner in a dark cell with no hope of escape.

Emotions may seem to be in direct conflict with one another. You can experience a wide range of feelings within the same day. This may add to the confusion at first as you sort through your situation. It's important to remember that situations change. One of my favorite scriptures for moments like this are the words "and it came to pass."

Giving Your Grief A Voice

Grief and emotion need a healthy voice. Without expression, grief is like a pile of dynamite waiting to be ignited. You need a voice. This book will help you give your grief and your emotions the voice that they need and deserve. Emotions will come and go. Their intensity will vary. In time, the emotional swings will be less frequent and less intense.

Giving your emotions a voice is necessary for healing the wounds. You may be a spouse who has been robbed of her voice. There are many different ways to express your grief. It's important to know what type of a griever you are. Some will think of grief rather than feel it. It may run through your mind but not be given an avenue of expression. This is where most spouses are when they begin the journey. Some will express their feelings through words, tears, and physical activity. You were created with a voice for a reason. Trauma in your life has tried to silence you. Part of this journey will be finding safe ways to express your feelings and grief.[10]

As you develop an emotional vocabulary, realize that there will be different intensity with each feeling you experience. A good exercise is to journal about each word. When I was feeling hurt and depressed, I journaled that it felt like I was moving in slow motion. I had no energy to pick up my feet and move across the room. The depression and grief was so overwhelming that I couldn't function. One spouse writes that her hurts felt like someone had surgically opened her chest without anesthesia, cut her heart out, and left her wide open without sewing her up where she could be trampled over and over again.

You may want to use visualization or imagery to help you express your grief. For me, it's a movie that helps with emotional expression. When I was a teenager, the youth group at church went to see the movie "The Hiding Place" when it was released. The story of Corrie Ten Boom and her family paying the price for the sacrifices they made had a lasting impression. The imagery of being tormented with unrealistic expectations, cruelty, and the horrors of concentration camps stays with me to this day. The second time I saw the movie I was in college. It was the weekend that Corrie Ten Boom passed away. I will never forget the closing line of the movie. "No matter how deep your pit, God's love is deeper still." The image of trying to crawl out of a pit and being wounded more as you struggle to survive gave me a way to express the pain and depression I was experiencing.[12]

Physically, you may experience weight loss as you go through the shock of disclosure. Some of the spouses in group call it the S-Anon spouse's diet. I've seen men and women lose anything from 10 to 30 pounds in the initial weeks of recovery. It's not the way you want to lose weight. I've experienced the weight loss that can come with depression. It's not the type of diet you want. Emotional eaters will typically gain this weight back as they return to food as a coping mechanism.

We may try to cope with these feelings with denial, drugs, alcohol, smoking, excessive eating, shopping, intellectualizing, or trying to "fix" the addict. These are temporary ways of delaying the pain. Stuffing feelings won't make them go away. When we accept these emotions and give them a voice, we take back our power and begin healing the painful feelings.

Your feelings during this time may begin to connect with past trauma. The majority of spouses have sexual, emotional, physical, or spiritual abuse in their past. The impact of trauma is more devastating than you might have previously imagined. This is a time to begin healing old wounds as well as new ones.

Finding safe people is critical at this point in the journey. This may be difficult to do in the pain of the crisis. One of the issues we will look at later in this book is that spouses of sex addicts don't necessarily have the best track record when it comes to picking safe people.

My Friend Is The Spouse Of A Sex Addict - How Can I Help?

Thank you for caring enough about the spouse of a sex addict to read this section of the book. You may be the first person that she comes to for help when it feels like the world is falling apart. One of the most important things you can do is listen empathetically and be available when the spouse needs to talk. Simply showing up and being emotionally available is a powerful way to care for a spouse.

More than anything, the spouse will need compassion. Love them with the love of God throughout their journey. Psalm 136 reaffirms God's compassion at the conclusion of every verse. Reaffirm your compassion for the spouse when you are listening, sharing, and simply crying with her during the nightmare she is living.

Be patient during her time of grief. Don't try to set a timetable. Let her experience her journey through grief on her timetable. Don't pressure her to restrict her process of grief. Each situation and person is different. Spouses of sex addicts are trauma survivors. When a parent or loved one dies after an extended illness, the process of grief has begun for the individual and family long before the person dies. With a sudden loss or trauma (discovering your husband's sexual acting out), the crisis of grief lasts much longer.[13]

Don't quote scripture at a grieving spouse. How many times have you heard Romans 8:28 read by well meaning people. Or maybe it's words like "suffering produces perseverance, perseverance produces character, and character hope." (Romans 5:3-4). A grieving spouse may feel like throwing her Bible across the room. The hurt, shame, and anger that come from inappropriate timing of scripture can harm her faith. There are no magic words, Bible verses, poems, or cliché's that will miraculously take away the pain. The spouse's circumstances are a nightmare that she is living through. Walk alongside her and be a supportive friend.

Don't try to fix your friend. This is a journey that the spouse must take or her wounds won't heal. She will be terrified as she faces things she would have never imagined in her marriage. Walk with her through those fears. You can't take away what she has experienced. You can be a powerful instrument of healing as you support her in this journey.

Coping with the emotions and feelings of devastation will be a critical element in the healing journey. You may feel somewhat drained after reading about grief. The good news is that this isn't the end of the story. It's only the beginning. This is a journey of hope, healing, and transformation. The grief and pain can be redeemed.

Chapter Two

Trauma and Betrayal

T he two most comforting words in the English language are "me too." Knowing you are not the only person on the planet who has experienced betrayal and trauma is comforting. That's why we are sharing Rhonda's story with you. She and I have walked in your shoes. We can relate intimately with your trauma. We know what it's like to experience suffering that is beyond words. So, why share her heart breaking story? Because even when it appears there is no hope for marital recovery, a trauma survivor just might surprise you. It's important that you read this story through to the end. This is a journey that has hope.

Rhonda's Story

In a split second, my sense of reality was destroyed. Life would never be the same. The moment of discovery left me devastated. It was as if I had been raped in front of a crowd that cheered on the rapist. The humiliation, shame, and pain were beyond words.

I had no idea my life would be torn upside down. I was told how loved and appreciated I was on a regular basis. I thought we had a great relationship and that things were wonderful. We regularly shared our love for each other and felt like we were best friends. You could have knocked me over with a feather when I found out the truth.

The grief, embarrassment, pain, humiliation, damage control, financial cost, and emotional disorientation are too much to bear. You are cruel. I know of no other way to say it. You are cruel. To fake a friendship and embed yourself in sacred spaces is sickening.

And to think of all I did for you. I meant everything I said. You obviously were lying the entire time. And I'm sure you are proud of yourself. Others have now told me that you made fun of me behind my back, rejoiced over the pain you have caused, and are proud of yourself for destroying me. You cost me my job and damaged my career and treasured relationships. I trusted you with my heart and my secrets. You broke every promise you ever made.

I don't know how I can recover from this. The level of betrayal, and the cruelty of your mindf***ing games defies anything I've seen in all of my years on this earth. You love inflicting pain and humiliation. I misjudged you completely. You have no conscience. To fake a friendship through my father's and best friend's deaths and then pull a cowardly stunt like this is sickening.

I gave you the very best I had. We were a great team. It could have been greater. The worst part is, I still love you. And I'm so **** loyal that I want to restore our relationship. I miss your touch and the comfort and feeling of safety it brought with it. You fooled me – it was only an illusion. I loved just sitting and talking with you over dinner. I loved sharing dreams with you. I loved working and playing with you. I had so many things I wanted to share with you – so many questions I wanted to ask. I learned so much from you.

The pain you have wreaked upon the entire family has devastated us all. If I had to choose between being raped again or going through what you have done to me, I would choose the rape. It was less painful and healed much quicker. I will never trust anyone again. I've had enough. Last night I went to something that should have been joyful for me. I watched our daughter perform in her first children's musical. It was about relationships in the body of Christ. I wanted to stand up and scream "It's all a lie. Don't get close to anyone. Don't share your heart. It will be destroyed!"

I saw someone last night who told me about Sheila being in the hospital. Her surgery went wrong. She can't sit down and she can't stand up without intense pain. There is no place of relief. She has no place to land. I feel the same way.

I have nothing to compare this to, and I can't absorb it. I've never been through anything like this. I just wanted you to sit down face to face and tell me why. We were always able to talk about anything. Everyone keeps telling me "you can't process what you don't know." They are right. You win. You whipped me and I know you enjoyed it.

I'm starting to see the impact on my faith. I had no idea I had fallen so far. I didn't think I was upset with God at the time. I guess I was and still am. All of the spiritual issues are coming up for me. The emotional pain still screams. I want to scream. Writing about God is scary to me. I feel so weird. Like he's here, but that I'm unimportant. I remember praying with you and how healing that was. I now doubt God and I can't even connect with Him. My faith is destroyed. I guess you got what you wanted. I'll do what I have to do to keep you from walking on me again.

I'm fighting to concentrate. I caught myself zoning out a lot today. It was hard to stay focused. I hope making some notes will help me do better. This dissociative stuff stinks. I was having memory lapses from the trauma of dad's illness, death, and other painful losses. People have come and told me things about myself that I have no memory of. I'd just like to heal.

Going forward this week is frightening. The inside is leaking through to the outside. I feel dark clouds every direction I look. I'm feeling whipped and defeated in so many ways. I'm so suspicious to the point of paranoia. I don't want to live this way. It's all so unfair and unjust. I hate to keep desperately clinging to illusions of hope which provide no guarantees. Somehow I have to rise above all of this.

I had another nightmare about you. I followed you through town. I shot at you, but the bullets went right through you and you weren't affected at all. It kept happening over and over. The bullets never stopped you. It happened over and over again. I realized you weren't human. I woke up and just prayed that you weren't from the same human race as the rest of us. I've been plagued with these nightmares for over a year. I wonder if they will ever stop.

I reached an all-time low. For the first time in my life, I know what it means to have genuine hatred for another human being. I would like to see you suffer as much pain as you inflicted on me. I pray that God will remove you from this planet. I've never felt that way about another human being. The worst part of this experience is that I now know the meaning of genuine hatred. I'm disgusted with myself and with you for doing this to me."[14]

Intimacy Carries a High Risk

"I made a royal mess of my life during that first year," Rhonda admitted. "I couldn't trust anyone. I felt suspicious of every 'friend' I had left. I couldn't open up to anyone. As the song says, I began 'looking for love in all the wrong places.' I wish I had sought help earlier in the journey. To his credit, my husband did. (The conclusion of this story will amaze you.) After almost eighteen months of depression, suicidal thoughts, isolation, and hatred, I finally decided to trust a therapist (Richard). I had lots of doubts, but was desperate and had to do something. I had lost almost everything I had worked for in my home and career. I had nowhere else to turn."

As "Rhonda" shared these words with me, I couldn't help but cry with her. Actually, crying isn't a strong enough word. I balled, wept, and sobbed uncontrollably. I've known these experiences personally, and I've seen them in my work with spouses of sex addicts. My wife isn't an addict, but these words come from someone who knows the devastation of betrayal and humiliation. I have heard many spouses say they can deal with the truth, but not the deception and dishonesty. The truth is painful. Feeling deceived, betrayed, and humiliated is traumatizing.

"My trust in people had been severely harmed," recalls Rhonda. "I trusted a close friend who had been with me through other betrayals, constantly affirming me and assuring me that it was their 'stuff' and not me. I should have learned not to rely on one person to help me through times of depression and anxiety. She would betray me and cost me a job that I had loved for so long."

The others were supervisors, church leaders, and two Christian counselors. Breaking promises, breaching trust, repeating things shared in confidence, all to hurt me. And they succeeded. I obviously can't pick friends.

Is it any wonder that I would marry someone who would cheat on me? As I've gone through treatment, I've begun to realize I'm not to blame for his choices. I'm not to blame for his cruelty, infidelity, deception, and lying. I could probably deal with just about anything, but the lying is the worst part. If he had told me he had cheated and wanted to get well, it would have hurt horribly, but I could have coped. The constant lying is what has broken me."

Relationships are risky. When you choose to share your heart with someone, the joy of being connected in a relationship is inspiring. When that relationship is violated, the result will boggle the mind and crush the heart. Intimacy carries a high risk. The pain of betrayal becomes impossible to capture in words. What do you say when the person you have trusted with your heart has deceived, betrayed, and psychologically tortured you? In the moment of crisis, explanations aren't heard.

As you saw in Rhonda's story, she disassociated herself with the reality she was part of. "At times I think I lost touch with reality," she shares. "The therapist used the word "dissociative" to describe feelings of splitting off from reality. It was a safe escape. I still struggle with my memory about these times. I have had so many nightmares during that time that I sometimes struggle to know what happened and what took place in my sleep."

As the spouse of a sex addict, you are a trauma survivor. Your wounds must be treated with the best care available. In one of our earlier sessions Rhonda said, "I believe I will survive, but as a walking amputee."

Now when I ask Rhonda if it was worth the pain, she answers yes. In fact, she insisted that I include in this book that she and her husband have been part of individual counseling and therapy groups. He is now over a year sober and they are at a place where they have decided to commit to the marriage.

In spite of the pain, there is hope for the journey. Many spouses such as Rhonda have worked through the trauma and are finding new life. The final chapter in your life and relationship isn't finished. Your story is still being written........

Chapter Three

Wounded: Heart, Soul, Mind, And Spirit

"**D**iscovering that I was married to a sex addict has made me feel vulnerable and crazy. I had just accepted so many of my hurts from the past as normal. Taking this journey has shown me that there is a much saner way to live. My trauma (I never thought I'd be able to say I had trauma) in my past has begun to heal. I now understand why my husband and I got married. I wanted him to heal me, and he didn't have a chance. And I learned I couldn't fix him either. Learning this has been liberating."

Margaret

As you begin reading this chapter, stop for a few moments, take a deep breath, and invite God to lead you into a clear understanding of what you need to take from these words. As you read, realize that these concepts may bring up difficult feelings. If this happens, you may need to explore these issues with a therapist. You may be able to talk through them with a safe friend in your support system. Make sure that you take care of yourself emotionally as you continue reading.

Why is the subject of past trauma important? Because the way you have learned to manage trauma will impact the way you cope with new trauma. The discovery of your partner's sexual addiction is a major trauma. Looking at your past trauma is for your own healing. It doesn't mean that you are responsible in any way for your partner's choices.

The word "trauma" brings up images of horrible abuse. The typical image is news stories of blatant physical and sexual abuse. To see evidence of this you only need to read the morning newspaper or tune into a major news network. Rarely does a week go by that a story of physical or sexual abuse isn't reported. This may not be the case in your life. Trauma may be single horrific events. It can also be a series of smaller events that impact your life over a period of time. Nancy Andreason defines trauma, as "Intense fear, helplessness, loss of control and threat of annihilation."[15] Rhonda's story reveals the feelings of shame, humiliation, and being annihilated. Bessel Van der Kolk gives a great description of the impact of trauma.

"One of the first things you need to ask is, how did you survive this? This is amazing that you're still here. It's amazing that you still have the guts to go on with your life. What is allowing you to function? What are you good at? What gives you comfort?" [16]

Trauma doesn't always come from inside the family. The news media tells stories of school teachers getting involved sexually with students. Day care centers have come under investigation for inappropriate treatment of children. Stories of kidnappings and child exploitation are too common. As a counselor, I hear many stories of abuse that was perpetrated by neighbors, babysitters, bullies, and family acquaintances. Trauma can also come from natural disasters. We live in a world that is experiencing a war on terrorism. One can be a victim of trauma that doesn't originate within the family of origin.

Whenever a new group begins for addicts or for spouses, we talk about the concept of "the wounded self" as a part of the cycle of chaos. In beginning a journey of healing and recovery, it's important that you become keenly aware of the impact of different types of wounds. This chapter will give an explanation of the various types of trauma that people experience.

Experiencing some form of trauma goes with life for most people. From a theological perspective, we live in a fallen world. Different forms of trauma have existed since the fall of man. From Genesis to Revelation, each book of the Bible contains examples of different types of trauma. The Joseph story in Genesis, the book of Job, and the life of David are a few examples of the suffering man can experience. The ultimate example of trauma survival is Jesus. He experienced the wounds of invasive trauma through physical beatings and ultimately the cross. Consider the other types of trauma that Jesus endured. In the garden of Gethsemane prior to his crucifixion, Jesus experienced being let down by friends. He experienced betrayal from Judas. He knew the pain of loss when he experienced grief with Mary and Martha over the loss of their brother, Lazarus. These are just a few examples of how the Son of God experienced different types of trauma during his existence as a human, living in a fallen world.

The experience of discovering that a family member has a sexual integrity issue is traumatic. Dr. Barbara Steffens has discovered in her research that 70% of spouses, upon disclosure, develop symptoms of post traumatic stress disorder (PTSD). Regardless of whether the addiction was discovered by the spouse or disclosed by the addict, the level of trauma remains the same.[16] During this time you experience the feelings of being violated, betrayed, and vulnerable to being hurt again. Chances are this is not the first time in your life you have experienced these feelings. Living with the impact of sexual sin impacts the family. You, your spouse, and your children will all be affected by our sexually invasive culture. Living with excessive amounts of sexual stimulation can produce traumatic experiences.

As we explore the issue of trauma, I want to share parts of my own story as illustrations for different types of trauma and how people can heal from these wounds. I will also share how these experiences from childhood and adolescence carry over into adult years. Trauma inhibits child development. The voice of the child is silenced or shut down, relationships are disrupted, and the role of victim begins to develop. Treatment methods will also be considered.

Types of trauma

Trauma encompasses more than physical and sexual abuse. Trauma may also be emotional and spiritual. One of the most frequently quoted statistics from the research of Dr. Patrick Carnes, involves trauma and sexual addicts. From this research it was learned that 97% of sexual addicts have experienced emotional abuse, 76%

were physically abused, and 81% were sexually abused. *It was also learned that 81% of spouses of sexual addicts have experienced sexual abuse.* Dr. Carnes work didn't include the category of spiritual abuse as it would be difficult to quantify for the purpose of clinical research. From experience, I can tell you that spouses and addicts experience spiritual abuse. The concepts of spiritual abuse will be addressed more directly in a later chapter.[18]

Like many in the helping professions, I have struggled with codependency throughout my life. People-pleasing and conflict avoidant behavior have led me into many problems. These have arisen from childhood experiences which profoundly impact adult relationships. Several of my childhood traumas were inflicted by female authority figures who were supposed to be responsible for care and safety. As an adult, I have found myself in relationships where I have been harmed by female authority figures. I also experienced during teenage and young adult years situations of spiritual abuse and as an adult, I have trusted church leaders who ended up hurting me and my family. As a child, I was physically beaten by bullies on many occasions and as an adult, I allowed myself to be taken advantage of in a variety of situations. As a child, I coped through isolation. It took many years of therapy and practice to bring me out of my shell where I could interact with other adults without fear and anxiety.

Invasive trauma

What is invasive trauma? It includes physical, emotional, sexual, and spiritual trauma and can take many forms. These are usually direct and invasive, and clearly impact people in negative ways. They will manifest themselves in different forms as young people transition into their adult years.

Physical abuse will take the form of assault upon a person's body. Hitting, slapping, pushing, shoving, and other forms of intimidation involving bodily contact, inflict physical trauma on one's personhood.

One form of physical invasion that I experienced came at four years old. I had a teacher who believed in old-fashioned kindergarten. She believed that a teacher should never smile. She ruled by fear and intimidation. One way in which she intimidated me was during snack time. Occasionally the school would serve tomato juice, a drink I didn't like. The teacher would call her student teachers to my side and have them physically grab my face and hold my mouth open while she forced tomato juice down my throat. This was a form of physical abuse coming from a female authority figure who was supposed to be responsible for my safety. Keep this in mind as you read other examples in this chapter.

Another type of physical abuse during this era came from a babysitter. A family friend was in charge of caring for my sister and I on a Saturday evening. During this time, she became angry with me and strangled me in my bed until I could barely breathe. I remember locking myself in my bedroom the next time I saw her.

Trauma doesn't always come from inside the family

Emotional abuse can take the form of yelling, screaming, name-calling, and any form of verbal abuse. An old saying goes "sticks and stones may break my bones but words will never hurt me." Words hurt the heart and soul of a child in ways that "sticks and stones" are unable to touch. Physical wounds can heal in obvious ways. Emotional wounds may take years to heal, and memories can always bring back the pain.

Bullying may take the form of physical and emotional abuse. I grew up as a victim of different forms of bullying. From first grade through high school, I was made fun of by students and ridiculed over physical features. Because I refused to fight back, I was vulnerable to physical beatings. I experienced many of them during these years. The church taught "turn the other cheek," so I never fought back. I remember on more than one occasion, lying down in a fetal position with people beating me, while doing nothing to protect myself. I believed that I had no control over my mind or body, and that people could do whatever they wanted to me.

The victim of the bullying is often blamed or punished for being a victim. If the victim seeks help, they are ridiculed by teachers and administrators who are supposed to be responsible for maintaining a safe learning environment. The isolation and loneliness that result can be devastating. "Ignore it and it will go away" didn't work. I tried it for 12 years and it failed repeatedly. This was during the era where teachers used public ridicule to humiliate students who didn't perform as expected. I went to school many days wondering how I would survive, and sometimes went days at a time without speaking to anyone at school.

As would be expected, I experienced academic difficulty with schoolwork. In elementary school and often in high school, female teachers would decide to make an example out of me, often by comparing me to my younger sister who was much more successful academically. This drove me deeper into fear, shame, and isolation.

I share this with you to show that one form of trauma leads to difficulty functioning which may lead to more trauma and more difficulty functioning. It was a vicious cycle that was extremely difficult to break. As I've worked through many of these issues, I've noticed the connection. One traumatic event would lead to another. Once trauma impacts your life it will carry over into areas that are unrelated to a specific traumatic event.

Sexual abuse covers behaviors such as touching or penetrating the genital area, teasing about the body, and inaccurate information about sexuality. This may come from strangers or acquaintances. A more devastating form comes from people in authority. When pastors, school teachers, medical professionals, counselors, and others who are responsible for maintaining safe boundaries in a relationship violate people sexually, they create additional trauma for people to overcome. I've worked with many women who were victims of the clergy. The trauma is devastating.

Peers can be difficult on children and teenagers during their years growing up. Sex education is not an option. The only questions are who will provide it first and who will give the most accurate information. You may have grown up in a family where there was a "no talk" rule about sex. Consequently it may be that you were involved in a discussion about sex with your peers, said something inaccurate, and were completely humiliated.

Today children are educated by a sexually invasive culture. Forms of sexual abuse may have invited themselves into your life. From accidental exposure to pornography, sexually explicit advertising, or rape, your sexuality may have been violated by some element of culture that you were not responsible for. It may be that you have spent years blaming yourself for something you had no control over. Sexual abuse robs you of your voice and power.[19] It may be that you suffered in silence and never told anyone about your experience. Or it may be that you attempted to seek help from a parent or another authority figure, only to be blamed or not believed. Sexual abuse, in any form, is devastating and must not be ignored. Professional treatment is essential if the impact of sexual abuse is to be overcome.[16]

Think back to your first experience with sex education. Was it from a parent, friend, magazine, book, the church, or school? What messages did you get? Were they positive or negative? The first experience I remember in a sex class was in 9th grade Physical Education. The teacher was not the type of person to be giving students their first exposure to sex education. To give you an idea of what she was like, we had a student who was born with a hole in her heart and this teacher made her run laps until she coughed up blood. This was the first person to formally teach me about sex. She was extremely invasive and inappropriate with the content of her class. She played tapes of graduate level lectures about sexuality for freshman in high school, and used unethical techniques for teaching her subject matter. As a student, I couldn't comprehend the course material and was unable to interact appropriately with my peers. Terms were used that I didn't understand and I was often laughed at for withdrawing when students engaged in sexual talk.

Later during this same school year, I experienced sexual abuse at the hands of a student teacher. I realized that I would never be believed if I had told anyone, so I kept silent for many years. The next year, a number of students at the church I grew up in had inappropriate sexual experiences with the wife of a church leader. And much of the inappropriate behavior took place in the church building. Sadly, I was among the victims. The fact that this occurred in a church setting also made it spiritual abuse. As the years moved on, there were other adult women in this church who were sexually inappropriate with me. Because I wasn't educated in even a basic way about sexuality, I never knew to call this sexual abuse. All of these situations involve women who were in authority and were responsible for maintaining clear boundaries.

I've since learned of the sexual acting out among people in this church who were leaders at the time. They were the most influential in my life during my teenage years. Some were involved in making and viewing pornography. At least 3 engaged in extramarital affairs. Others were involved in going to strip clubs and hiring escorts. Is it any wonder that this church environment was ripe for sexual abuse? And these were all church leaders.

As you read these examples, are you starting to see a pattern? Read on.

Spiritual abuse can take the form of messages about an angry and punitive God. It might be that there are negative messages about sex that come from the church. Or it could be that you experience some form of physical or sexual abuse at the hands of a church leader. A church in the Atlanta area made national headlines a few years ago when they were ritualistically beating children in their Sunday morning worship hour. Many viewed this only as physical abuse. The fact that it took place in church makes it spiritual abuse. One victim of sexual abuse shared how her father would pray while raping her at night.[20] When people go to a pastor or church leader in crisis, they may emotionally be looking at him as the presence or voice of God. When people seek help from a Christian counselor and are abused in some form, this becomes spiritual abuse. My first therapist called herself a Christian counselor. She was licensed by the state and saw clients in a church building. I had never been to therapy before, and it would take 2-3 years to discover that this therapist was abusive through her inappropriate self-disclosure and poor boundaries. She led me to believe the relationship was something other than a professional one. She revealed many deep personal things she had experienced, and played right into my codependency. Our first session was more about her broken marriage than my issues. Many of our sessions were more about her than me. There was great psychological and spiritual abuse in this relationship. Upon disclosing it in group therapy years later, people commented on how they felt like I had been raped. Anytime a relationship involves spiritual things or titles, there is the potential for spiritual abuse.

Wounds of Abandonment & Neglect

Trauma isn't always blatant and obvious. It may take a subtle form. Trauma can also appear as neglect and abandonment. It may be that physical, emotional, sexual, and spiritual needs were unmet or devalued. This can leave a desperate sense of neediness in your life. People will look to fill these needs in many ways including addictions.

Physical neglect can involve being left alone without proper supervision. It could be that there was not adequate food, clothing, or shelter. Health and medical needs may have been neglected. I have had clients who were never taught basic hygiene. They had to be taught the basics of self-care because these behaviors were never taught or modeled. Being left alone as a child has created wounds. One spouse that I work with was left alone for hours after school every day in elementary school. She experienced people trying to break into her apartment. At one point her mother left her alone in a wading pool. She looked up and an alligator approaching, but there was no one to call for help. Being left alone before one is mature enough to manage it can bring trauma.

Emotional abandonment is seen regularly in spouses I work with. It may be that you were not heard as a child. Learning to listen and being listened too is very important. Perhaps no nurturing or caring was directly expressed. Or it may be that the only emotions expressed were negative. It may be that positive emotions were never modeled.

Spouses struggle with emotional dishonesty, which may have been learned from emotional abandonment and neglect. How often have you told someone that everything was just fine when you felt like you were dying inside? Have you ever told your husband/wife that you weren't angry, when you felt like you could punch a hole in the wall? If you lie to yourself enough about your emotions, eventually you will get to where you believe the lies, and the pain will become even greater and more confusing.

It may be that you came from a family that never expressed affection. Your parents may have come from an era where your dad said, "I told your mother I loved her 50 years ago and if I change my mind I'll let her know." This can lead to emotional neglect. Were there ever pats on the back in your family? Was appropriate physical touch modeled? Hugs? Affirmations? All of these are important in child development. Hospital nursery's make sure that infants are held on a consistent basis. If a child is not touched and affirmed in appropriate ways they experience a condition called "failure to thrive."

Sexual neglect takes place when there is a failure to provide proper sex education. Intimate relationships need to be modeled by parents. The term "intimacy disorder" is used to describe sexual addiction. The disease of both the addict and spouse is an intimacy disorder. Intimacy, however, is about much more than sex. Perhaps you didn't observe real emotionally intimate encounters while growing up. Perhaps you saw people being emotionally dishonest. Maybe your family pretended there was nothing wrong when you knew there were serious problems. Were people being real with each other? What picture did you get of intimacy from significant people in your life?

I have been conducting a survey of sex addicts for the last year. One question on the survey involves sexual abuse. It lists several forms of sexual abuse and asks each man to identify the ones he has experienced. The number one form of sexual abuse that has been listed has been lack of accurate sexual information. Did you come from a home where there was a "no talk" rule about sex? I talked about how a physical education teacher attempted to force a group of freshman to learn about sexuality with invasive teaching techniques. The next year we had a new physical education instructor. He refused to tell us anything. Instead, he showed a film or had a guest speaker come to class each day of sex education week. The message that was sent was that sex was a subject that is too embarrassing to talk about. Sexual invasion and sexual abandonment are both unhealthy extremes. The ditch on one side of the road isn't much different than the ditch on the other side of the road, as one of my colleagues is fond of saying.

Spouses may end up looking for intimacy in the wrong places. This is when the roles of martyr and rescuer are used. Spouses may emotionally kill themselves in search of intimacy. These feelings of desperation may have contributed to you entering a relationship with an addict. Addicts attract martyrs and rescuers like an extra powerful magnet. Needy men will attract women who will try to take care of their needs at all costs.

Spiritual neglect is harder to identify. There may have been a failure to model spiritual disciplines or a failure to present a picture of God that includes love, acceptance, and grace, which will impair spiritual development. Addiction treatment models, and many other mental health issues, acknowledge that there is a need for people to accept a power greater than the madness. For Christians, this can be defined as acknowledging the lordship of Christ. Failure to teach and model spirituality can result in feelings of loneliness and neglect. The need for spiritual community will be discussed in a later chapter.

Through these descriptions it can be seen that trauma can take different forms. The issues of invasive trauma are the most obvious. The issues of neglect and abandonment are equally devastating, perhaps more so since they are harder to identify. As I look back over my own life, I see both forms of trauma at various stages. Notice that the illustrations I used did not directly involve any family members or relatives. And yet, these events profoundly shaped my development. As you think about the illustrations I have shared, notice that there is a significant pattern of abuse from female authority figures. A babysitter, student teacher, school teachers, church leader's wife, and others, resulted in relationship issues throughout my young adult years. As I reflect on these events which shaped my development, and consider the last 20 plus years of adult life, I can see how these early experiences created patterns that I had to work hard to break, but there is hope. These patterns can be broken and the cycle of trauma and abuse doesn't have to go on to the next generation.

Healing Traumatic Wounds

So what can I do about trauma? After reading about these manifestations of abuse, you have to wonder if it is possible for anyone to get well. What is the healing process like? Is it possible to survive the impact of trauma in my life? The answer is yes. We have a God who heals; and he has given us many resources on this earth to facilitate that process.

Professional counseling can provide healing resources. Properly trained therapists have a number of techniques that can be used to facilitate healing. Resources for finding a therapist are found in the resource list at the back of this book. I have seen God work in the counseling process in ways that are amazing. Trauma is ultimately a tool of evil that God can redeem. Some trauma treatment can only be done in a safe, professional setting.

Journaling and letter writing can help with processing traumatic experiences. As you experience trauma triggers (things which remind you of a trauma) you can process them in your journal. This is your document. It is sacred. Nobody else should read what you write. It is for your healing, not someone else's. Letter writing can be a way to confront a person or situation in your past. You should NOT initiate a confrontation with an abuser without professional help. Ultimately, the battle will have to be won in your mind. This is where an abuser continues to victimize, even if there hasn't been any exposure for years.[21]

To magically state that forgiveness is simple and takes place in an instant is to drive the victim deeper into devastation and anger towards God.

Forgiveness is a concept which has been greatly abused. The misconceptions will be addressed in the chapter on spiritual abuse. Forgiveness, properly understood, is a powerful tool for healing trauma. As I'm writing these words, Centennial Olympic Park bomber Eric Rudolph has just finished his sentencing trial in Atlanta, Georgia. One of the victims spoke of how she had found healing in her ability to extend forgiveness. This is a powerful story that can be misunderstood. Forgiveness is a process, not an event. It is a process that will be repeated many times. The victims of Rudolph's reign of terror will not get to a place of forgiveness without many long nights of agony and grief. Forgiveness is not a magical moment in time. It is a long painful process that can bring healing. Forgiveness is short-circuited when the process is interrupted, minimized, and devalued. To magically state that forgiveness is simple and takes place in an instant is to drive the victim deeper into devastation and anger towards God. When forgiveness can be exercised as part of resolution to the grieving process, it can heal the wounds that have kept you enslaved.

Support groups are critical to your recovery as a spouse. Sharing trauma will help you reclaim the power that was lost to physical, emotional, sexual, and spiritual abuse. A group provides a source of comfort, support, hope, and strength. It's a place to express yourself and give voice to the feelings that have been repressed. It's a place to share your journey with others. You may have more than one group during your recovery. It may be that you need to hear the stories of people who are struggling with the same issues you are. During the times when you are struggling with emotional pain and memories, you will need others to lean on.

Telling your story will help take the power out of the trauma. Secrets are enslaving. They hold you hostage and lead to physical and emotional difficulties. Sharing your story in safe settings will decrease the amount of energy it takes to keep the secret. Telling your story also encourages others in your group.

Revisiting your story as an adult. One of the things that has helped me with my journey is revisiting the places where the abuses took place. PLEASE NOTE: This is something you only do when working with a trauma therapist. Do NOT try this without proper support and guidance. In 2004, I made the decision to return to Cape Girardeau, MO and spend some time visiting the places where much of the abuse took place. To go to those places as an adult where I couldn't be harmed in the same way was powerful. It was a time of release as I went to each place, prayed for those who had harmed me, and experienced things as an adult. My memories had involved intense feelings of victimization. I had lived as a victim in so many ways. Experiencing those places as an adult who couldn't be sexually abused by past perpetrators provided new perspective on myself, and the wounds of the past.

I've talked with people who were in the church where the abuse took place. Learning more about the people, and the context has helped make peace with the past. A small number of leaders were sexually acting out and engaged in making sexually explicit videos. Yes, my faith has been affected. At times it is up and down. Experiencing the outrage, and compassion of people who have learned of the spiritual and sexual abuse has been healing. Trauma survivors often remain silent for fear that they won't be believed, or out of fear that they will be blamed. I'm grateful to the people who have been willing to walk with me through this experience.

Since the first edition of S.A.R.A.H. was released, I've had more healing experiences around the trauma of the past. The most notable was the night before the book was released when I shared these experiences with my parents for the first time. I wish that everyone could have the experience I had that night. It was through a phone call as we live hundreds of miles apart. There was no blaming, only blessing. Their statements were affirming and supportive, and their questions completely appropriate. I'll never forget my dad praying for me on the phone that night and feeling so blessed as his son. It would be less than a year before my mother would pass from this life. I felt that the last year of her life was the best in so many ways. I believe that it was the experience on the phone that night that led to some of the healing that needed to take place.

Others have since reconnected with me via facebook and other means. We have been able to share stories and experiences. I am convinced that no matter what the wound, trauma, or addiction, one of the most powerful things you can do in your journey is to share your story with someone. It is sacred and important, simply because it's yours. It doesn't matter if people don't agree with you, or accept your perspective. It is valuable because it is yours.

In 1935 a movement began that has saved the lives of millions of people around the world. June 10, 1935 is known as the beginning date of Alcoholics Anonymous, a 12-step movement that now exists all over the world. It began with two men sitting down to share their stories with one another. I'm not a diehard supporter of 12 step groups, but I love the wisdom of their traditions and literature. The simplicity of being able to connect with other people in the pain, struggle, and hope of their personal story has been phenomenal. And it's something that any human being can participate in, as one who shares or as one who listens and connects.

Get to know your story and the power of sharing it with others. It may be the most healing thing that you do as you take your journey of recovery as the spouse of a sex addict and trauma survivor.

Finding meaning in pain will be where you begin to see the redeeming power of God at work in your life. Meg (name changed) came to me after discovering that her husband had returned to his affair partner for the second time. She and her husband had been married 27 years and raised two children. She accepted him back after his first confession. Ultimately he chose to go back to his addiction leaving Meg devastated. She came to me in a state of profound grief. We worked together for a year. During this time, her pain began to heal. She then began working with other women who had experienced unfaithful husbands. I have seen many clients through the years who came through Meg's home on the way to my office. She found hope and meaning in the pain she had experienced. She saw God's hand of redemption in her life as she shared the healing journey with others. It has been a long journey for Meg. As difficult as it has been, today she wouldn't trade the results for anything.

Pain is ultimately what unites us with others. It is when we share the painful parts of the journey that bonds of intimacy are deepened. Galatians 6:2 tells us to carry each other's burdens. Notice that it doesn't say that you are to martyr yourself and carry everyone's burdens by yourself, while you pretend that everything is ok. Failure is the one word that unites the entire human race. Whether you experienced trauma, addiction, or any other struggle, we all know what it is like to fail. Relationships are deepened when the hurt, pain, and failure that you experience can be shared.

My Story

As I've traveled through the memories, pain, and grief that went with the traumas I've shared above (and many that I didn't have space to share), I have used many of the above techniques and many more. Journaling was a way to process thoughts and feelings that I was unable to share with others. This was a safe place to process during sleepless nights. A support group for people who had experienced spiritual abuse, was also a critical part of the journey. Sharing the experiences with others showed me that these traumas could be survived. Forgiveness was an extremely difficult concept for me to grasp because it was closely tied with spiritual abuse. With the help of a therapist, I was able to confront an abusive female therapist who had inflicted a lot of hurt. This was structured in such a way that forgiveness eventually resulted, though it was many years coming. Finding a small group of people that I could be completely honest with helped eliminate some of the shame that dominated my identity, and having a number of people I could call as I battled debilitating depression, literally kept me emotionally and spiritually alive. Medication gave me the ability to function so that I could do the hard work of therapy. Brain imaging can show you how depression impacts the brain. PET scans, FMRI imaging, and SPECT imaging are providing new insight into brain functioning, especially as it related to depression, anxiety, attention deficit, and addictions. While the science is new, it is amazing how the images can show how medications work in powerful ways.

Today we have methods for trauma treatment that weren't readily available when I was beginning this journey 15 years ago. At a later point in time, I went back to my therapist to do some deeper work. I discovered the power of things like experiential therapy, eye movement desensitization reprocessing (EMDR), guided imagery, and forms of art therapy. Through some of these techniques, I was able to utilize parts of my brain that weren't exercised in cognitive therapy. These are all techniques that can only be used by properly trained therapists. Since going through trauma therapy, I have been amazed at the physical and emotional impact it has had upon my life. I haven't had one bad blood pressure reading (after years of medication to keep it under control) and many physical problems have virtually disappeared. Obsessive thoughts have been calmed and many relationships have been restored. The journey hasn't been perfect. It has come with many long, painful nights of tears. God has been redeeming my pain, just as he did with Meg.

I've learned through these experiences that I couldn't walk with people who were broken until I was broken. I couldn't share their pain until I had experienced it. I know what it is like to face the dark, hopeless pit of depression. During these times, you find out who your friends are. Some are still with me 15 years later. People I once judged as weak, are now people I respect. The "magical fix it God" concept has died a long needed death. God heals in his time, not mine. He strengthens people and enables them to survive difficult journeys. God never removed Job's pain, but he did empower him to endure to the end. Perfectionism has been replaced with patience and tolerance, as people have struggled through painful times. The cold silence of isolation has been replaced with warm, caring, intimate friendships with people who are willing to walk through pain.

Nothing will change your theology like recovery from trauma. No adult who has lived through the journey of recovery from trauma will ever be able to worship the God of the flannel board in Sunday school.[22] Your relationship with God will deepen and you will know him in ways you never dreamed possible. God will become real to you. You will feel his presence, care, and concern for you as an individual like never before. I believe that I experienced genuine conversion to God during trauma treatment. He is *Rapha*, the God who heals. The God I worshipped before facing the pain no longer exists in my life.

The God who heals people's hearts and spirits is someone I see in my office on a daily basis. Invite Him into your pain and let Him transform it into a ministry. You will experience His presence as never before.

Conclusion

So what does this have to do with your journey as a spouse? The traumas of the past impact the way we respond to the discovery of new trauma. As you face the reality that the knight or princess you married has fallen, you will begin experiencing new trauma. The feelings you experience may trigger memories of wounds that existed long before you met the person you married. There are patterns in past hurts that can provide valuable information for current healing.

Sometimes we replicate past trauma in current relationships. We keep repeating patterns trying to heal the wounds of the past. Maybe you are trying to find that magic person who will heal all of your past hurts. As you can see from my story, it doesn't work. I continued to find people who would hurt me. One reason I encourage all spouses to work on their own issues before making a decision about staying in the marriage, is that if they don't, the likelihood is high that they will end up in another destructive relationship. Even when spouses vow to never marry again or to never have anything to do with the opposite sex, it still happens.

After a minimum of a year of intense work, I would then encourage you to consider making a decision on the relationship. When the time comes that you decide to stay, let your spouse know that you are making this commitment to a new relationship. Don't make this decision quickly. Decisions made in the midst of grief will be second-guessed and usually regretted. Go through the grief, learn all that you can about yourself, and then commit to a journey of healing.

Chapter Four

How Did I Get Into This Mess?

One of the most difficult things spouses face, especially at the start of the journey, is being able to take their focus off of the addict and begin to look inward. We marry the people we marry for a reason. People who get into harmful relationships accept the myth that if they leave the abuser, it's ok to enter another relationship. It's the idea that "I was deceived and got tricked. It won't happen again." Before long, they find themselves in a relationship with another addict or someone else who will hurt them. Perhaps this time they have gone from a marriage of physical abuse to one of emotional abuse. In other words, they have not changed. It's the same problem with a different presentation. Until the "victim" begins to look inward and identify his/her own areas of responsibility, the cycle of destructive relationships will continue. *IN NO WAY DOES THIS MAKE YOU RESPONSIBLE FOR THE CHOICES OF THE ADDICT IN YOUR LIFE.* This will be explained further in this chapter. Part of the journey of healing will be to consider how your wounds and family of origin patterns contribute to the cycle. One of the greatest challenges a spouse has in recovery is to look at these issues without blaming themselves for the choices of their partner. One goal in your journey is to break the cycle in your life and in the lives of your children. This can be done even if your partner chooses not to get well.

This chapter will look at some of the issues that keep spouses in this destructive cycle. These include the factors that get a spouse into a relationship with someone who has sexual integrity issues, and the things they are doing to keep the cycle fueled.

S.H.A.M.E.

Self

    Hatred

        Accepting

            My

                Enslavement[23]

Nothing fuels a cycle of self-destruction like shame. Shame may be deeply rooted in the environment in which you were raised and its resulting trauma. As the acrostic suggests, shame involves self-hatred.

The belief that I am a terrible, worthless, unlovable human being will create the belief that "I deserve what is happening to me." For Christians, the concept of shame may be reinforced with scripture and religious tradition. Hymns with phrases like "for such a worm as I" and messages from pastors and teachers may reinforce self-hatred and the belief that "I'm experiencing pain as punishment for being so terrible." Shame is the difference between making a mistake and *being* a mistake. Shame-based thinking reinforces the belief of worthlessness.

Is Shame Always A Bad Thing?

Someone once said, "Memory lane is a great place to visit, but you don't want to take up residence there." Shame is somewhat the same way. Shame can be the result of a conscience that is under conviction. Brokenness and humility are hallmarks of recovery. We certainly wouldn't want a spirit of pride around the behavior that has led you and your partner into this journey.

Shame and honesty are mutual enemies. An honest assessment and confession of the reality of the pain we are experiencing, and accepting personal responsibility for your part in the relationship, will do more to heal you from unhealthy shame than anything else. James says "confess your sins to each other and pray for each other *so that you may be healed.*" (James 5:16*a* emphasis mine). Have you ever wondered why God tells his children to confess their sins? It's not like he doesn't already know them. We aren't feeding God new information when we share our weaknesses with him and others. The purpose of honest confession and acceptance of personal responsibility is for our own healing. Saying something out loud takes away the power of the secret. There is much wisdom in some of the old sayings of Alcoholics Anonymous. One of these sayings is, "You are only as sick as your secrets."[24] When something is said out loud, we hear it. It becomes less powerful and more manageable. I have heard many spouses through the years talk about how the shame was lifted when they shared their own personal story with others who were walking the same road. We will talk later in this book about the critical importance of healing in community. A writer named, Albert Ellis, wrote about overcoming shame and the importance of shame attacking exercises.[25] Sharing your story with others is the greatest shame attacking exercise you can ever do.

How do we go about making changes and not get caught up in unhealthy shame? Judas gives us an example of where unhealthy shame can lead. Upon realizing the seriousness of betraying the son of God for 30 pieces of silver, he went into a field and hung himself (Matthew 27:5). Peter also betrayed Jesus, but had a completely different response when he was faced with that reality. Peter demonstrated humility and was willing to make changes in his life. Peter also teaches us that this is not a onetime event. Throughout his ministry, there were times when he had to be called back to the attitude of humility. We are all on a journey that has ups and downs. Sometimes it is more like an emotional roller coaster with hills and valleys of different lengths. Paul tells us that "Godly sorrow brings repentance that leads to salvation and leaves no regret, but worldly sorrow brings death." (2 Corinthians 7:10) Shame will ultimately lead us into an identity smothered in shame that leads to more shame. It does not bring about change. However, a small amount of healthy shame will lead to conviction, honest self-examination, and sharing with a mentor, accountability partner, or member of your support system. Spouses need mentors and support as much as addicts. This will be addressed further when we discuss healing in community.

It may be that shame has been deeply engrained in your life. This self-hatred leads to an acceptance that I am enslaved to my belief system, the messages of my family of origin, and other significant influences in my life. The acceptance of abuse as normal endangers people's hearts, lives, and spirits.

An addict will often unite with a shame-based partner. This happens because the addict is also shame-based. In the course of his/her addictive rituals, the addict may use the shame-based thinking of the partner to manipulate him/her into believing that he/she is responsible for the addict's sexual integrity issues. This happens because the addict cannot face his/her shame alone and so it may be projected onto the spouse. The shame-based spouse will internalize these messages, often with lightning speed. It's easy since it simply affirms the messages of shame and humiliation that the spouse has felt long before entering into the relationship.

Recently I completed a study of spouses who attended our groups and workshops, utilizing the Carnes-Delmonico trauma index.[26] This instrument looks at eight different types of trauma reactions. In analyzing the significant scores, the only area that men with sexual integrity issues and spouses had in common was trauma shame. If you look at the Carnes cycle of addiction, shame is at the core.[27] Shame and secrecy are the gasoline that fuels the engine of unhealthy dependence on substances, relationships, and behaviors. Shame issues must be addressed in order to lay a solid foundation for recovery.

The messages received from family of origin may contribute to shame-based thinking. The messages from pastors, school teachers, and other significant figures in your life may have helped create and encourage a destructive cycle of shame. I have given up on labels like "healthy and unhealthy families" and "functional and dysfunctional families." All families have healthy and unhealthy qualities. All families have functional and dysfunctional traits.

The fact that we are considering family of origin issues may have already created a shame-based response. Perhaps you feel the need to make your family look good, or not negate the positive things that happened in your history. It may be that a strong sense of shame and a fear of disloyalty are creating some anxiety as we begin to look at these issues. In a fallen world, nobody is exempt from bringing baggage into marriage and other adult relationships. It goes with the territory of being human. No family, school, or church is perfect. An honest assessment of these issues can be a great asset in laying your foundation of recovery.

Family Ties

Years ago I was relating a situation involving a very distant family member. You might say that he was the "black sheep" of our family (a very distant relative). Many of us had been embarrassed by the public nature of this man's business dealings. I found myself going out of my way to make sure that people who knew I was a distant relative also knew that I did not approve of, support, or participate in any of this man's activities. Shame and fear were strong factors in my choices.

You are born into your family of origin. This is not something that you had any say-so about. As I was freely sharing this story, someone spoke up and said, "I guess you can't choose your relatives." Shame leads us to try and take responsibility for things we have no control over, namely other people's choices. Blaming your family will not help you overcome shame. Living as a victim is a choice you will make. Victor Frankl emphasizes the power of choice throughout his writings.[28] To give up the power of choice is to submit your life to the control of others. It's a decision to live life as a victim. While we have no control over who our relatives are, we can control our choices and make a decision to abandon the role of perpetual victim.

Your family, regardless of what role they have played in your life, is the source of many of your values and beliefs. Some you have adopted and some you have rejected. Even if your family was physically and emotionally absent, messages were still sent. As you begin your journey, consider what these messages were and how they have shaped your heart, mind, feelings, and perceptions. Challenge any messages of shame as you are considering these things. When you are tempted to feel disloyal to your family, or believe that you are doing something wrong by addressing these issues, remind yourself that you are not blaming your family for your problems. You are looking at patterns that can help you heal your wounds and prevent past mistakes from being repeated.

Family Rules

All families have them. But rarely are they ever spoken. You typically don't know they exist until you unknowingly break one of them. It may be that the rule is discovered when you tried to talk about a difficult subject and everyone in the room went silent for a moment and then changed the subject. It wasn't stated that you couldn't talk about the issue at hand, but the message was communicated loud and clear.[29]

Don't Talk . . .

about sex, religion, politics, death, or any other subject that is uncomfortable. You may have been taught to avoid bringing up any subject that makes the family look bad. We "don't talk" about uncle Joe serving time in jail. Or we don't mention the sibling that dropped out of high school. It's the belief that, "If I keep the secret, it won't hurt as badly and maybe it will go away." The "don't talk" rule is one of the most common with spouses. Have you ever been in one of those conversations where the room goes strangely silent? Someone has just broken the rule. People are figuring out how to change the subject to avoid the anxiety.

We create these rules as ways to cope. Raising the issue of sexuality in a home where sex is never discussed can bring about intense messages of shame. Talking about a family member who died may make people anxiously change the subject to avoid coping with their own grief. The things that the "don't talk" rule often applies to, are issues we don't know how to fix.

Yes there is a time and place for talking about difficult subjects. A family without boundaries will talk too much and give inappropriate details to people who aren't safe. There are times when it is safe and appropriate to speak freely about difficult topics.[30] Other times are not appropriate. Learning to tell the difference may be difficult if appropriate boundaries haven't been modeled. Finding safe people to discuss important issues, through which you may have experienced shame, will be invaluable in your journey towards healing.

Don't Feel

Feelings may have been ridiculed or ignored. Somehow the message gets sent that you shouldn't feel certain feelings. A variation on this rule may be that you only experience positive feelings that the family knows how to manage. As the spouse of an addict, you may have ignored many warning signs because of the "don't feel" rule. Things may have been extremely uncomfortable for you when you discovered something painful or were asked to do something that you couldn't support. Feelings may be ignored if you have not had your feelings validated.

Emotional detachment can lead one to accept dangerous consequences. Spouses may have developed a high level of pain tolerance if they have been taught that their feelings are shameful. The human body is created with feeling for a reason. It involves protection and survival. You experience feelings of pain and hurt which warn you of potential harm. If you touch a hot stove, you feel pain. This is a warning to move quickly away from the source of the heat or risk long-term damage. In the same way, emotional pain can warn of threats to your spiritual and emotional safety. These feelings need to be felt, validated, and considered carefully.

One spouse I worked with was in such denial about the validity of her feelings that she would continually tolerate physical, emotional, and spiritual abuse from her husband. She was willing to ignore his 15 years of sexual acting out with prostitutes, strangers, and members of churches which he had pastored. She believed that if she could just maintain a higher level of commitment, maybe her nine children wouldn't be affected by the family in which they were being raised. She has developed such a high tolerance for pain that betrayal has been normalized. In her family of origin, she was taught that feelings can't be trusted. The message she reported from her family was, "If you feel something negative then you are obviously wrong."

Male spouses may have been taught that, "Big boys don't cry." To feel pain and express it with tears may bring an extra dose of shame and criticism. Statements like, "Quit crying or I'll give you something to cry about" or "Go to your room and don't come out until you stop crying" may have reinforced the "don't feel" rule.

An old saying goes, "You can't heal what you don't feel." This is true when it comes to spouses in recovery. Learning to feel allows you to experience the range of emotions that God intended when he created you. Jesus experienced a wide range of emotions that we see in the gospels. He experienced grief, sorrow, exhaustion, anger, and joy. Consider your own emotional range. Perhaps there are feelings you are avoiding because of the "don't feel" rule in your family of origin.

Denial

"It never happened." "Ignore it and it will go away." "Nobody else noticed anything." Denial is crazy making. It's the hippopotamus that is pooping in the living room that the whole family ignores. They will go over, under, and around the animal to avoid dealing with it directly. Maybe there was an addict in your family of origin, but nobody would ever admit it. Growing up with denial will make you tolerate things that are unhealthy while denying their existence. It will eventually cause you to question your own reality. It amounts to lying to yourself so much that the lie becomes your truth.

Blame

"It's not my fault." Addicts and family members project blame onto others. It's the denial of personal responsibility for one's actions. Blame perpetuates the victim role. It prevents healing from taking place. Ask the questions "what can I do to improve my situation?" and "what am I responsible for?" Modeling responsibility is part of breaking the cycle in your family.

Appearances and Reputation are Everything

This is the family that always looks good when dressed up in their Sunday best. Everyone behaves just right when they are in public and never tells the family secrets. This family may have people who overcompensate for their addictions, conflicts, and other struggles by becoming overly involved in religious activities. To the outsider, everything looks wonderful. The family may even be praised in church or the community as being role models. The outside of the cup is clean, sparkling, and shiny. The inside is full of pain, hurt, and a longing to be heard and validated.

Minimize

What is minimizing? Minimizing is one of the most insidious family rules that can exist. It creates confusion and a lack of self-trust. It normalizes the bizarre and creates a high tolerance of unhealthy pain. Minimizing pain and emotions leaves one vulnerable to extreme hurt. It includes statements like, "It's not that bad." "Nobody else was bothered by it." Or, "It's no big deal – everyone else is ok with it." One spouse writes, "I had a perfect childhood even though my parents died when I was young." How can you have a perfect childhood when your parents died when you were a toddler? This is the statement of someone who has coped with pain by minimizing their feelings of hurt and grief.

Minimizing feelings can take place through the comparison trap. By saying that my pain isn't as bad as someone else's, I invalidate my own experience and minimize the hurt. The comparison trap leads to minimizing difficult emotions and experiences. Comparing yourself to another person has only two possible conclusions, and both of them are bad. You either wind up looking down at someone in arrogance, or you develop a feeling of inferiority and minimize your own experience. This leads to identity confusion, the inability to make decisions, and a lack of self-trust. Spouses like this have a difficult time voicing their opinion because they have been taught that their opinion doesn't count. They will try to avoid giving input for fear of being wrong. They will try to figure out what they are supposed to say and think rather than give honest expression to their ideas and identity. They will downplay their own experience.

This is not an exhaustive list of family rules. These are common in the spouse's family of origin. Other rules might include beliefs such as, money is the most important thing in life, reputation is everything, don't upset dad, children are to be seen and not heard, and many others. Take some time and try to identify the rules that existed in your family. Remember, you are doing this exercise for yourself. The purpose is not to send you back to your family of origin to give them a lecture on everything that they did wrong. You are doing this to understand the issues that went into creating your current situation. Ultimately, you are doing this to make an honest self-assessment and to help break the cycle for the next generation.

Family Roles

Part of coping with family rules and trauma involves adopting different roles in your family of origin. These roles are developed to cope with family rules, trauma, and life in general. As we work through this section, remember that we are looking for extremes. Some of the roles and rules can have healthy aspects. Ecclesiastes 7:18 remind us, "It is good to grasp the one and not let go of the other. The man who fears God will avoid all extremes." Consider some of these roles that might have existed in your family of origin.

Addict

It may have been a parent, grandparent, or another relative. The addiction may have been sex, drugs, alcohol, work, religion, food, relationships, or another substance or behavior. Regardless, there was something present that you were aware of, even if you didn't have all of the details as a child.

The addict may be loud and boisterous while acting out, but on the inside they feel angry, hurt, lonely, frustrated, and guilty. They may experience low self-esteem and struggle with maintaining a job and relationships. If they have picked a socially acceptable addiction, like work or religion, they may be getting positive reinforcement for acting out. It may be validated with promotions and praise. The drug addict, alcoholic, and sex addict might receive more direct and severe consequences over time. Others may remain caught up in their addiction for longer periods of time because they get some of their needs meet from the praise and feeling of pride. The entire family may be living a lie, but the addict will do his/her part to keep the system going.

Martyr (Enabler)

This is often, but not limited to, the spouse of an addict. The martyr will take extreme levels of emotional, spiritual, and sometimes physical abuse believing that they will one day rescue their partner from his/her addiction. A martyr will tolerate lies, being blamed for the addicts problems, and will enable the addictive behavior to continue. Addicts love to marry martyrs who refuse to get into recovery. It keeps the addictive family system functioning and makes maintaining an addiction easy for the addict. As long as martyrs do their job, addicts don't have to look at their own issues and can continue to "medicate" their own pain. The martyr eventually ends up feeling a lot like the addict. Anger (usually turned inward), hurt, loneliness, frustration, guilt, and low self-esteem describe the inner experiences of a martyr.

The martyr believes that if they can please the addict and take care of his/her needs, then the addict will eventually change. There is an element of narcissism in being a martyr. Deep down, the martyr believes that he/she will come out a hero for saving or rescuing the addict from their disease.

When I was in graduate school, our psychopathology teacher decided that the students would benefit from doing a ride-a-long with a police officer on a night shift. He believed that we would observe psychopathology first hand in this exercise and was he ever right! That evening I learned lessons that could never have been taught in a classroom. I rode with an outstanding police officer from the Atlanta police force. This was the week of the second Rodney King trial and we were patrolling the part of town where the riots had broken out during the first trial. The city was on high alert for possible violence. As we left the police station, the officer said something to me that I have never forgotten. "Richard," he said "When the time comes that we are involved in a fight or a shootout, the one thing you have to remember is that you don't ever try to be a hero because nobody will remember it tomorrow. You will wind up dead, the other person gets away with what they are doing and they go right on and do it to somebody else." This is what martyrs do in relationships. They believe that if they destroy themselves emotionally, spiritually, and physically, then they will somehow be glorified and save the other person. The reality is that the addict or abuser ends up barely noticing. They go right on and do it to someone else. An addict can always find another martyr.

When the martyr is the spouse, they may be suffering from relationship addiction. One of my favorite shows was "Knots Landing." During one episode, Gary had experienced a relapse with his alcoholism. Valene is turning over every rock in the city of Knots Landing trying to find him. In frustration, she drops on the beach with her neighbors right behind her and says something like, "Why is it that everyone thinks his addiction to that bottle is so bad when my addiction to him is worse." This is how spouses of addicts try to cope. They may be throwing themselves into a relationship to avoid having to face their own pain or feelings of inadequacy.

When the martyr begins to change, the addict will resist. This is a good sign. It may be that you are setting boundaries for the first time in your relationship and enforcing them. And you may be experiencing growing pains. But understand that resistance isn't always a bad thing. I have heard many addicts say after years of sobriety that it was their spouse's willingness to state boundaries and enforce them, which blessed their recovery immensely.

Hero

The hero (sometimes called, Golden Child) is typically a first born child. Some variations of this role are the little Prince/Princess and the Saint. This is typically the overachiever. It may be the "good kid" on the block. This is the child that may become a pastor or enter a helping profession. The hero may have been successful publicly and the family may have used this child to make the family look good. Or maybe he/she is the athlete that wins awards for their achievements. The hero is trying to overcompensate for perceived inadequacies. Like the martyr, the hero believes that if he/she can perform well enough, then the situation will change and their needs will be met. Emotionally they feel guilt, hurt, inadequacy, and may become very resentful. Heroes are often perfectionists. This is based on the perception that if everything is done "just right" that everything will be ok. A hero might one day become a scapegoat if they get frustrated enough. It is common to play more than one role in your family and roles may change over time.

Scapegoat

The scapegoat is sometimes called the problem child. This is typically the member of the family who is rebellious and defiant. They may get into substance abuse, have legal problems, and become violent. This is the child who is taken to the therapist. The family tells the therapist to fix the child when in reality it is the family that needs therapy. In actuality, the scapegoat may be the healthiest member of the family. They see the problems in the family and shine a light on the dysfunction through their behavior. Family members don't want to see these problems so they focus on the scapegoat. Rebellion isn't always about doing things that are harmful or illegal. It could be that the family has three generations of doctors and the unwritten rule is that the children must enter the medical profession. The scapegoat could choose to rebel against the system by choosing to be an auto mechanic. The family system may have a hard time absorbing this type of a change.

The scapegoat experiences feelings of insecurity and fear. They are lonely, unsure, and have an intense fear of rejection. They will try to control their environment by force in order to feel connected to people. All behavior communicates something. The behavior of the scapegoat may be a dramatic cry for help. Due to the level of rejection they have experienced, it takes a long time to earn their respect and develop trust.

Mascot

The mascot may have a reputation for being the family clown. This is a role that may bring praise and other forms of positive attention for a period of time. But eventually it becomes annoying. The mascot is attention seeking through humor and being "cutesy." The mascot functions as the emotional thermostat of the family. A thermostat keeps the temperature within a comfortable range. When the atmosphere in the home gets tense, the mascot may crack a joke and lower the intensity. They may be the family cheerleader. When things get down, the mascot may raise the mood with a performance.

Some studies have suggested that the mascot has a high likelihood of developing suicidal tendencies. Internally, the mascot is fearful, insecure, tense, anxious, and frightened. Humor becomes a way to cope with feelings of inadequacy. The story is told of a man who went to a psychologist many years ago for treatment of depression. The psychologist recommended that he go to a show by a comedian at a local club. The man protested and stated he couldn't do that. When the psychologist asked why, he responded, "Because I'm that comedian."

If you find yourself cracking jokes as a way of minimizing pain, you might have learned to do this in your family of origin role as a mascot. It becomes a socially acceptable way to cope with uncomfortable situations. Sadly, it is a way of swallowing pain and becoming depressed. Mascots need to be challenged to be honest with their feelings. They also need a strong support system as they face these feelings, perhaps for the first time in their lives.

Lost Child

The lost child is isolated, lonely, and often forgotten. Maybe you were the child that was left out of activities. Or perhaps your name was forgotten. Or you got left at the restaurant and nobody noticed for a period of time. I knew one "lost child" who was left at the bank and the mother didn't notice the child missing until the bank president appeared at her front door with her six year old daughter. A lost child is typically sad and quiet. They experience strong feelings of rejection, loneliness, and abandonment. They rarely express their feelings verbally and may suffer in silence for years.

It's easy to understand how a lost child might survive in a marriage to a sex addict for a long period of time. The spouse suffers in silence because they feel that they have no voice. Their role as lost child creates the belief that they have no significance. Lost children may retreat into isolation and deny feelings of betrayal and pain. Their level of tolerance is high and they may suffer in silence for long periods of time. They are taken advantage of and often exploited.

Support and therapy groups are helpful to lost children. Bringing them out of isolation and empowering them is therapeutic. The lost child will need help identifying emotions and learning appropriate forms of expression. One lost child I worked with had detached from her feelings to a dangerous extreme. She couldn't say no to any request from her husband. No matter what she felt or thought, she complied without protest. Eventually she allowed him to abuse her physically to fulfill his sexual fantasies. It took coming to the point of near death to realize how serious her situation had become. Her feelings had been rejected as valid long ago. She suffered in silence for many years before beginning her journey of recovery.

This is not an exhaustive list of roles. Think carefully about different roles you have experienced in your family of origin. Did they change over time? Which ones have you played? What roles did other family members play and how did they interact with you?

And Then Comes Marriage

"Two people don't get married. Two families send out scapegoats to reproduce themselves."[31] When you think about family rules and roles it is important to look at yourself first and take your own journey. Marriage is a uniting of the rules, roles, and other baggage of two individuals who come together. Nothing exposes secrets like marriage. Expectations are shattered and disappointment sets in. Rules get violated and role conflicts begin.

I discovered how family rules could impact a relationship early in marriage. Shortly after moving to Atlanta, Vickie had a wreck one night and our car was totaled. We had been frustrated with our American-made cars spending excessive time in repair shops and we began looking at foreign-made cars. Things went great until it came time to make the decision. I was enthusiastic about owning our first Honda Accord. As we got closer to closing the deal, however, I noticed Vickie began to waiver. She had an intense fear of rejection from her father about buying a foreign car. He was a veteran of World War II and had spent the rest of his career with an American manufacturer of cars. I discovered quickly that there was an unwritten family rule that said, "We don't buy foreign cars" in this family. It was so powerful that Vickie literally feared being disowned by her father over this decision. Nobody had ever come right out and told her she couldn't do it. And yet, it was as if someone was holding a gun to her head threatening to kill her if she broke this family rule.

"Two people don't get married. Two families send out Scapegoats to reproduce themselves"

The family I came from had two rules about cars. Get something that functions well and buy it for the best price you can possibly get. When it came time to buy the Honda, we had two family rules come into conflict. The most functional, efficient car we could find was the Honda, but that didn't matter in comparison to a potential rejection by a father. You can imagine the feelings and struggles that followed this and other conflicts, as we began to realize what we each brought into our marriage. I began to feel that I wasn't special and that my wife devalued me. She began to feel like she had to choose between me and her dad, all over a car. I could go on and on, but I believe this illustrates how two family rules can create a conflict.

We choose the person we marry for a reason. It is not an accident that you selected your spouse. Many of us were looking to a partner to heal the wounds that had been ignored for many years. Disappointment sets in when we discover that there is no single person on the planet who can heal every wound from our past. Part of the journey of couple's recovery involves looking at the baggage you bring into your relationship and how it interacts with your spouse.

When you realize that you are married to someone with sexual integrity issues, there is that moment of devastation in which you ask yourself, "How could this have ever happened to me?" Through the examples given of rules and roles, you can begin to see how you might have been attracted to an addict. More importantly, as you understand the roles you have played in life, you can identify changes you need to make in order to have a healthier relationship with your spouse.

This is a basic look at how our individual issues impact our marriages. Couples recovery is a separate issue deserving of a longer book. *"The Sacred Space"* is a weekend retreat conducted by Faithful and True Marriages that addresses couples recovery. Resources will be listed at the end of this book. For now, continue to focus on your own issues as a spouse. Your journey of healing is critical whether the addict in your life chooses to get well or not.

Chapter Five

Spiritual Trauma:
Has God Abandoned Me?

*Debbie had begun to see unusual behavior in her husband Jim.
He had started coming to bed later each evening. Whenever she
came into the room and he was on the computer, the screen suddenly
changed so that she couldn't see what he was doing. She decided to
learn about the computer and begin checking his Internet history.
Debbie found that Jim had spent hours visiting sexually explicit web
sites on a daily basis. She began reviewing credit card statements
and discovered that there were charges for telephone chat lines.
Feeling devastated and humiliated, Debbie didn't know where to
turn. Should she keep it to herself or seek help? Debbie decided to
go to her pastor for advice.*

Debbie made an appointment with her pastor. She went to his
office and shared what she had discovered. But she was surprised by some of the things the pastor had to say. He told her that
her searching Jim's computer and credit card bills were signs that
she didn't respect her husband the way God desired. He then asked
her about her own Bible study and prayer habits. When Debbie
said she could be doing better, the pastor implied that this might
be the reason why God was allowing her to go through something
so humiliating. He then reminded her that the last time he visited
her home, it was dirty. When Debbie explained that it was hard to

work, keep the house clean, and take care of 3 children, the pastor reminded her of how hard it is on a man to work all day and come home to a messy house without dinner prepared. He then asked if she was willing to forgive her husband and never say another word about what she had found. He also suggested that she try increasing the amount of sexual activity in the marriage, and reminded her that the Bible said she is to submit to her husband.

I wish that Debbie's story was unique. Unfortunately, I've seen this happen repeatedly with spouses who go to well meaning pastors for assistance. The spouse comes away blaming herself, feeling more shame and humiliation than before, and the cycle of destruction continues. The addict continues in his/her cycle and the spouse feels responsible.

In chapter four of this book, the concept of spiritual trauma was presented. The definition I will use for spiritual abuse is as follows:

Misuse and/or manipulation of the name of God and scripture, through position or teaching, in order to avoid consequences and project blame onto others. In Debbie's situation, the pastor was creating spiritual trauma through two methods. One was through the misuse of Scripture. The other was through his position as pastor. At some level, when a hurting person seeks help from a pastor or church leader, they are emotionally looking for them to represent the voice of God. Therefore the pastor's

Misuse of the name of God, through position or teaching, in order to avoid consequences and project blame onto others.

words will carry extra weight. Debbie left feeling like if she didn't conform to the pastor's suggestions that she would be disobedient to God.

Male spouses experience unique responses from church leaders. A man I worked with shared with me (as did one of the elders of his church) that if he could learn how to please his wife, she wouldn't have to run around on him. Another man was told by his pastor that women don't have problems with sexual acting out and that he must be exaggerating or have misunderstood something. He was told to simply "trust God" and that his marriage would be ok since both he and his wife were Christians.

Spiritual trauma can take a variety of forms. It can be direct and it can be covert. Regardless of the form, never underestimate the power of God's name and his word. The Bible describes the word of God as, "Living and active; sharper than any double-edged sword it penetrates even to dividing soul and spirit, joints and marrow; it judges the thoughts and attitudes of the heart." (Hebrews 4:12) A double edged sword can be a weapon of defense that can preserve life, or it can be a murder weapon. A knife in the hand of a skilled surgeon brings hope and healing. The same knife in untrained hands brings destruction.

History teaches us that wars can be fought in the name of God. Many lives have been needlessly destroyed in the name of God. In the Guyana Massacre in the late 1970's, people believed they were following the leading of God when they committed suicide. Charles Manson utilized the Bible in ordering the murders of many in the late 1960's.[32] Examples like these reveal that the name of God can be used in a destructive manner.

It is mistakenly assumed that spiritual abuse only takes place in groups exercising extreme mind control tactics or among religious extremists. Spouses who have been wounded spiritually will tell you that it happens in mainstream religious groups. I shared several examples in chapter 2 on trauma that illustrated how spiritual abuse can take place in normal evangelical denominations. When a parishioner is abused emotionally or sexually by a church leader or in a church setting, spiritual trauma has taken place. The view of God and the church have been altered by these experiences. When affairs take place between church members, the lives of the people affected will be spiritually altered.

Submission Texts

Arguably, the most abused words in the Bible are, "Wives, submit to your husband's as to the Lord." (Ephesians 5:22, Colossians 3:18) These words have been used by sexual addicts to explain to their wives that no matter how bad their acting out gets, the wife must always remember to submit to them. One spouse was told that if she didn't participate in her husband's sexual acting out in swingers clubs she would be violating the biblical command to submit to her husband. Another was told that if she wouldn't visit strip clubs with her husband and engage in exhibitionistic activities, she would be sinning. When asked if the command to submit included blatantly sinful activity, the husband told me that "God would honor her for her submission to me even if it was doing something wrong." Another addict explained to his wife in my presence that she had to accept his voyeurism (looking at women through a telescope) because he was the God-ordained head of the house and she was to submit to him no matter what. The manipulative nature of addict thinking is clearly revealed. The message is that if the spouse refuses to accept addict thinking, she is in rebellion against God. The use of Scripture becomes a means of control; instead of a source of power and conviction that leads to a life changing relationship with God.

Father Leo Booth writes, "Religious addicts manipulate with guilt. Who dares to argue with the Bible? Who dares not side with God? How can anyone object to a godly lifestyle? How can wanting your family to reap the rewards of heaven be abusive? When there is no balance, when religious addicts give their families no choice, when there is no room for differing opinions and beliefs, it becomes abuse. When they restrict their families lives, and continually trying to force them into a belief system under threat of rejection, punishment, or abandonment, it becomes abuse."[33]

Spouses are threatened with isolation if they don't conform. The use of the name of God creates a force that may be hard to overcome. It's hard enough to feel rejected by a family member. When it feels as though the rejection is coming from God, it's hard to make changes in your relationships. Many people experience performance-based religious groups, where failing to perform can lead to shame and isolation. The hurting inner child will fear isolation, abandonment, and loneliness; especially if the threat is perceived as coming from God. Irrational demands for submission can keep spouses off balance in their relationships and their spiritual perspective.

Isolation

Isolation is a technique used by addicts to keep spouses in the addictive family system. The spouse may be alienated from family and friends. An addict will use guilt, fear, shame, and other forms of manipulation, to keep the spouse from changing or leaving the marriage. As long as the spouse is jumping through the hoops the addict creates, the addict is enabled to continue their cycle and the spouse suffers in silence. As a spouse, you might have been told that the time spent developing close friends should be spent caring for your family. An addict won't like outside influences affecting their marriage. People may be perceived as threats and the addict will try harder to isolate their spouse.

The addict might use shaming statements regarding care of the children, condition of the house, quality of meals and lack of frequent sex, to keep the spouse in isolation. When you feel that love and acceptance must be earned through good works, the sense of duty may drive you deeper into the same system. Breaking free becomes difficult because the fear of more isolation is devastating.

Recently an addict came and told me how he kept his spouse isolated. He convinced his wife that it was sinful to take birth control pills. She kept having babies (9 at last count) and had to abandon all outside contact. He claimed special powers and messages from God as head of the house and she meekly submitted to his every desire. He convinced her that the problem was all his so that she wouldn't attend spouses groups and seek help for herself. Friends encouraged her to set boundaries but her belief was that God wouldn't allow her to question her husband. She continues to stay home and try to earn his approval while he continues in his freedom to act out in massage parlors with prostitutes. The tragedy is that she believes she must continue to tolerate this lifestyle or risk being in rebellion against God. And she is now pregnant with child number 10. Her husband continues to act out sexually while she remains on a farm in isolation.

Sexual Submission

Another section of Scripture that is abused, are Paul's words in 1 Corinthians 7. The first seven verses deal with the sexual relationship between husbands and wives. Addicts may misuse these verses in a selfish manner. The addict may be quick to remind the spouse that they are responsible for meeting all their sexual needs. However, the context of this chapter is mutuality. Husbands and wives share in responsibility. One doesn't lord it over the other. Selfishness isn't a part of Paul's words. The concept of mutuality is difficult for people who struggle with the trauma of not having their needs met early in life. The sense of desperation can lead to selfishness. An addict will act as a child who fears not getting his way.

Spouses who seek help from church leaders have found 1 Corinthians 7 used to blame them for the acting out of the addict. I have seen many spouses who were told that they could never say no to their husband because their husband would then be tempted to go outside the marriage. These spouses were taught that they must submit sexually to their husbands on the basis of these verses, so that their husbands wouldn't be tempted to sin. One church in the Atlanta area was regulating the number of times each week that husband and wives had to have sex. The reason that they gave was "so your husband won't be tempted to lust." The sex addicts in this church enjoyed this rule. It took responsibility for the husband's purity and placed the burden on the spouse. The spouse is in an impossible situation with this teaching. If she "gives in" and has sex she is humiliated and potentially subjects herself to disease as well as emotional danger. If she resists, it is as though she is in rebellion against God. The feeling of powerlessness and hopelessness is magnified.

One pastor's wife had gone to the church elders for help with her husband's extramarital affairs. These elders arrived at the door of her home with a box of lingerie from a popular store. She was told that she should wear these things, and that if she performed right, that she could "keep our preacher at home." In her devastation she tried it and felt more humiliated than ever. Sexual addiction isn't about sex. There isn't enough sex in the world to fill a hole that only God can fill. As a spouse, no matter how hard you try, you can't be God. The addict must assume responsibility for the choices made in sexual acting out.

Advice From The Clergy

As was stated earlier, the words of the clergy will be perceived by the person seeking help as the words of God. A study was conducted on women who had sought help from members of the clergy during times of trauma in their marriage. 71% reported dissatisfaction with the response of the clergy. They reported responses like the following:

"Stay and work things out. God expects that."

"Christians forgive and forget."

"Hope and pray for the best and God will change him."

"Try harder not to make him angry."

"He is hopeless and cruel but you are married to him."

"Cook better meals. Fix his favorite foods."

"Don't talk so much around him."

"All most men need is a warm dinner and a warm wife in bed."

"Wear him out with sex."[34]

Women who go to the clergy for help may experience the impact of misogyny (hatred or mistrust of women.) Churches tend to have male dominated leadership. And pastors who have unresolved trauma and issues with women may project this onto spouses who come to them for help. Another issue is that research indicates a high percentage of male clergy are struggling with sexual addiction issues. Without taking their own journey of healing, it is difficult for them to minister to spouses who are in crisis. One youth pastor came to me seeking help for a pornography addiction. He was trying to work with a number of his teens who had the same struggle, yet he hadn't overcome it himself. He wisely referred these teens to other professionals for help and began his own therapy.

Spouses are already questioning themselves when they develop enough courage to seek help. When members of the clergy discount or minimize their problem, chances are they will wind up questioning themselves again. Some of my clients have reported that their pastor would say things like:

"Don't worry about it. All men do this once in awhile."

"Try being a better wife and maybe he won't behave like this."

"Read Romans 8:28."

"Don't talk about your husband like that. He contributes to this church and is a great Christian leader. He wouldn't do anything like that."

"He may just be going through a phase. Keep praying for him and read your Bible more."

"It's probably not that bad. He will outgrow it."

"We don't talk about things like that in this church. Don't bring it up again."

"If I'd come to a house that looked like yours I'd have an affair too."

Sometimes the abuse from the clergy isn't so subtle. Recently a spouse came to me after experiencing difficulty with the advice from her church leaders. She and her husband had been placed "under church authority" because of his sexual addiction. Over the course of a year, the leadership never met with him once. He continued in his addiction. She and her children were blamed and ridiculed by the leadership in countless meetings. The children had been traumatized by the father while he faked his recovery. At one point, the father admitted to me that he had no desire to change. He enjoyed "chasing women" and intended to continue this lifestyle. His wife and children were directly blamed for being "too demanding" and not understanding the pressure on a father and husband. One of the children had broken down under the emotional pressure, and had broken a picture that belonged to a church member. The child asked for forgiveness and offered to pay for what he had done. The church leaders laughed at this 11 year old boy, told them he wouldn't be forgiven, and demanded that he pay $150 for the picture. Upon further investigation, it turned out that the picture only cost $12.50. The impact on the faith of this family has been devastating. We will talk about safe churches in the chapter in this book on healing in community.

Cliché Phrases

Nothing frustrates a grieving, hurting person more than cliché phrases. Canned theology at a time when you are trying to survive a crisis may drive you into an even deeper depression. These phrases are broad and general enough to contain basic truth. They also make an emotionally bleeding heart, bleed more. My friend, Mark Laaser, refers to this as "correct theology incorrectly timed."[29] The phrase may be biblically and theologically correct, but it may be that it's being used out of context or at a time when it is inappropriate. Words are powerful, especially when they come from a church leader. Words meant for healing may need to be used after emotions have been dealt with, losses have been grieved, and hope can begin to return.

"Just Trust God"

At the moment of disclosure, you probably aren't ready to trust anybody. Especially if there has been spiritual abuse and a feeling that God has let you down. The sense of pain and abandonment may be too strong at the moment. Trust will be rebuilt later in the journey. Being told when you feel the weakest that you need to trust more, will create resentment. Spouses hear this statement as an accusation that they lack faith. If they can't say, "I trust God" in the moment when things are worse, a guilt trip may follow.

"Just Pray About It"

This is rooted in the concept of a magical "fix-it" God. It's the idea that if I just say a prayer that God will magically take my pain away. God may have a purpose in mind for the pain. He may choose to allow it for your growth. The hidden message is that if somehow you have more faith, your prayers will be heard and God will fix your situation. Also at times of grief and loss, it may be that it is a struggle to trust God enough to talk to him. Questioning someone's prayer life in a time of grief and crisis will not deepen their desire to talk to God. Prayer in moments of pain may look different than it does on a clear day.

Prayer can be a wonderful part of the healing journey, however, spouses told to "just pray about it" are placed in an impossible situation. Again we can see where the spouse is placed in an impossible situation. If the addict doesn't suddenly get sober, it is communicated that it is because of the spouse's lack of faith. Your faith, no matter how weak or how strong, isn't responsible for the choices of the addict. Prayer is about a relationship with God, connection, and hope. When prayer is about building a personal relationship with God instead of a shopping list, it is amazing how your prayer life will begin to change.

"Forgive And Forget"

Forgiveness has been one of the most abused and misunderstood doctrines of Christianity. One of my group members called it "the "F" word of Christianity. Many people have been frustrated with phrases like "forgive and forget." This is a way of telling a hurting spouse to deny the reality of her situation, ignore her emotions, and pretend it never happened. It's a simplistic use of a phrase that dumps responsibility of reconciliation on the spouse. Addicts have ridiculed their spouses by assuming that forgiveness means that they shouldn't have to experience consequences, and things should return to normal upon confession of their addiction.

An illustration of the misuse of forgiveness was seen recently with a man whose children were physically and emotionally abused by his in-laws (the children's grandparents and uncle). Initially his wife stood firm, but shortly began wanting to take the children back to see their grandparents and uncle. She ridiculed her husband repeatedly by saying "if you would just forgive, everything would be okay. Mary was aggravating everyone and got what she asked for." The message was that the kids were to blame for the abuse they endured, and the father was now to blame for not "forgiving." Notice that the abusers were now free to repeat the abuse and bear no consequences for their actions.

Forgiveness doesn't mean that you subject children to repeated abuse, no matter who does the perpetrating. To do so would perpetuate the cycle of abuse for another generation.

Misconceptions About Forgiveness

Forgiveness is often presented as a simple choice. Unfortunately it runs deeper than a cognitive choice and it definitely isn't simple. Forgiveness is a process that doesn't need to take place quickly. It may be a "one day at a time" process. It involves wrestling with difficult emotions and making difficult choices. The decision to forgive will not quickly bring positive feelings. You will be doing better before you feel better. Making a decision to forgive will eventually bring you a sense of relief and hope. Good feelings often come long after difficult decisions are made. In other words, forgiveness is not a one-time event. It is a choice that will be made more than once in your journey.

Forgiveness doesn't mean reconciliation. I have worked with many spouses who felt pressure from their church or pastor to reconcile because the addict in their life had asked for forgiveness. Can you forgive your husband/wife without reconciling? Yes. If you own a business and an employee steals from you, can you forgive that employee? Yes. Would forgiving that employee mean that you allow him to keep his job? Not necessarily. Reconciliation will certainly involve a decision to forgive, but it will involve much more hard work.

Another misconception is that forgiveness will eliminate consequences. The damage of an affair will exist long after a decision to forgive and reconcile. Reconciliation involves rebuilding trust, identifying relationship patterns, and much more hard work. The consequences will be long term. There will be reminders that will take you back through the painful memories. Physical consequences from sexually transmitted diseases may exist long after forgiveness and decisions to reconcile. Recently, I met with a spouse who had decided to forgive her husband and reconcile the marriage years earlier. However, she still experiences the consequences of an STD due to her husband's choices. Her decision to forgive didn't eliminate consequences.

The idea that forgiveness must be accepted is another misconception. Forgiveness is unilateral. One purpose of forgiveness is for you to be released from the burden of bitterness and hurt. One of my favorite TV shows is *All In The Family*. During one episode, Archie has had an emotional affair and Edith has discovered her husband's infidelity. As they are standing on the porch, Archie is begging for a second chance and says to Edith, "Will you ever forgive me?" Edith replies that she had already made a decision to forgive, because if she didn't she would have to live with the bitterness and pain every day for the rest of her life. She then explains that her feelings are about the journey of rebuilding trust, dealing with the memories, and working on the marriage.

Forgiveness will be a critical part of the healing journey. It must not be treated as a trite religious phrase. The decision to forgive must be made from a desire to heal yourself. Forgiveness is largely for your healing. It must not be used as a way to inflict guilt and shame on those who are not able to reconcile their marriages. Church leaders need to handle the concept of forgiveness with care. A decision to forgive someone who has violated you sexually, emotionally, physically, and spiritually will be one of the most difficult choices you ever make. It's a decision that will be made many times as you grow in your journey of healing. It's possible that the addict in your life may never choose to receive forgiveness. Long after the decision is made, positive feelings will come.

A final thought, the more you realize how much you've been forgiven, the more you will want to explore how forgiveness can lead you into the freedom that Jesus died for. Jesus paved the way for reconciliation, but God never forced reconciliation on man. We have a choice to receive God. The addict in your life will have to choose to receive forgiveness from God, and from those who have been hurt by his/her choices. And you as a spouse will make your own decisions about reconciliation.

Conclusion

The words of pastors, church leaders, and any spiritual authority are powerful. Study them and question them carefully. Don't just assume that another human being (clergy or not) has any special access to God or his Word. You can take your own spiritual journey. Healthy and safe churches will allow you to question the words of any human being, including the pastor or board of elders and deacons. Develop your own relationship with God and your own personal faith.

As the spouse of a sexual addict, you will be in a vulnerable place when you walk through the door of the church seeking help. Fortunately, there are many safe churches and leaders who will embrace you and walk with you on your journey of healing. Don't give up – there is hope.

Chapter Six

Myths of the Journey
(with Joyce Tomblin)

Marriage is often a journey that people begin with fairy-tale expectations. However, the honeymoon ends when the myths are exposed and reality sets in. I'll never forget the devastating feeling at the end of the first fight my wife and I had in our marriage. Neither of us believed we would ever say and do the things we had done to each other. It was a fight over dealing with in-laws and credit cards, two fairly common issues for newlyweds. At age 22, Vickie and I were confronted with a reality that we weren't ready to accept. We began to realize that there were many false beliefs we brought into our marriage. Part of our growth was acknowledging the truth that we would begin discovering about ourselves and each other.

Your journey as a spouse will challenge your beliefs about life and marriage. This chapter contains some of the myths spouses have presented in our groups through the years. All willingly contributed to this book with the hope that others can learn from their experiences. Many of these myths have prevented or delayed spouses from experiencing their personal journey of healing and recovery. A survey was taken among some S-Anon groups in the Atlanta area of around 100 spouses. It was learned that the average spouse started their journey of recovery almost one year after the addict had begun attending meetings. A long grieving process can account for some of this, but the majority presented many of the myths in this chapter as a reason for not seeking help.

You aren't alone. Most spouses start their journey with false beliefs. It's our hope that you will be able to benefit from the experiences of others and not allow false beliefs to keep you from healing the hurts that you feel in the wake of betrayal. Challenge the beliefs that keep you stuck in a cycle of pain and self-destruction. Don't be ashamed. You aren't the only one who bought into the idea that you were to blame for something you couldn't control.

Myth #1:
This wouldn't have happened if I had been a better spouse.

Reality
Your spouse and others, including your family, friends or church, may initially blame you. You may get messages from them that you needed to be gentler, more loving, submissive, and sexy. These excuses are a sign of others' misunderstanding of sexual addiction. And they may be an attempt on the addict's part to avoid owning the addiction and taking responsibility for getting well. While you are responsible to your spouse for *your* behavior, you are not responsible for his or her behavior. Your behavior as a spouse is not what caused the addict's behavior.

Every person has his or her own faults. No matter how bad your secrets are or how many skeletons are in your closet, your spouse's addictive behavior is not justified. Many spouses who marry sex addicts have been sexually abused. As a result, shame and other consequences of the abuse keep them from believing their true value. Other hurts from the past can have the same effect. A fundamental part of healing as a spouse is dealing with your own secrets and hurts in a safe place. While our past can influence our feeling of worth, we need to be aware of our inherent value. Knowing our value can protect us from unnecessary self-blame.

Myth #2:
We must not be right for each other. If we were meant to be together, nothing like this would have happened.

Reality

Bad things can happen in any relationship. Read the Biblical story of Adam and Eve. Trials and struggles are opportunities to grow stronger.

According to Virginia Satir, it's not the problem that's the problem; it's how we cope with the problem. In our work with spouses, we've seen seemingly hopeless situations turn into vital relationships.

Myth #3:

My spouse doesn't want sex with me because I'm not attractive enough.

Reality

Sexual rejection doesn't mean that you don't measure up. Many spouses of sex addicts are very attractive and, according to their addict, "good" husbands or wives.

An addict may act out sexually instead of engaging in sex with a spouse because the sex addict fears intimacy and connection. Some addicts have experienced a past trauma that promotes the belief that for sex to be good it has to be "bad." These addicts may turn their sexual energy toward pornography, prostitutes, or affair partners. It is about the addict's intimacy impairment. It is not about you as a spouse.

Another reason for the lack of sexual activity by the addict can be sexual anorexia (acting in). Similar to anorexia nervosa, sexual anorexia is about control and power. Both types of anorexics will starve themselves in irrational ways when their needs could be met in healthy, legitimate ways.

It's important to remember that sexual addiction isn't about sex. Addicts are trying to use sex to fill holes that only God can fill. In a time of brokenness, one addict who had acted out with thousands of partners said that no matter how many partners he had, it was never enough. The story of actress Halle Berry and her marriage to a man she identifies as a sex addict, reveals that even when an addict is married to a beautiful Hollywood actress, it won't be enough to prevent sexual acting out.

Myth #4:

My spouse won't need to go somewhere else for sex if I become more sexual and do whatever he or she wants.

Reality

This assumes that you can control his addiction. In reality, it will have no affect on whether he continues to act out or not. Sex addicts have been known to have great sex with their spouse and still need to go masturbate in front of a computer immediately afterwards. This is not about him needing "too much sex." It is an intimacy disorder. Part of recovery should be learning what true intimacy is and is not. Sex outside God's design never fulfills. Eventually a neurochemical tolerance builds up and there is a progressive need for more acting out.

There is also the reality of sexually transmitted diseases. Since your partner has been involved in sexual acting out behaviors, we suggest you don't have unprotected sex with him/her. Insist that he/she receive testing for sexually transmitted diseases, and get tested yourself. One of the most humiliating and painful moments a spouse experiences is the trip to the family doctor or gynecologist to request a test for sexually transmitted diseases. There is the fear of wondering if the doctor believes it was your husband or you who acted out. Some spouses appear to be driven by the fear of rejection and the need for approval. As painful as this moment will be, it is necessary physically and emotionally for you to protect yourself and begin proper self-care. Spouses have been known to get involved in acting out with the addict when they believed this myth. We've seen spouses visit strip clubs, view pornography, and involve other partners in the marriage in trying to please the addict.

Myth #5:

Everything will be fine if we throw ourselves into the marriage and spend all of our time together.

Reality

As tempting as it may look, enmeshment is not the solution. Spouses need to develop themselves as individuals in addition to developing a life as a couple. Doing everything together may be an attempt to keep control of your spouse. The sex addict may also desire enmeshment, as it puts him or her at the center of the spouse's universe and feeds the narcissism that is typical of addiction. A healthy balance of connectedness and separateness needs to be present in the marriage.

No one has a perfect marriage. Every marriage goes through periods of too much closeness and too much separateness. One of the realities of marriage is that it is comprised of two wounded people taking a journey through life and recovery. Just spending time together isn't enough to cure the problem. True intimacy must be learned and practiced.

Myth #6:
I can fix whatever is wrong with my spouse.

Reality
Since you didn't cause the problem, you can't control it or cure it. One of the most difficult aspects of being in a relationship with an addict is admitting you are powerless over the addict. Some spouses take responsibility for making appointments for the addict. Addicts cannot get well by allowing someone else to do the work of recovery for him or her.

Your consistent attempts to affect the sex addict don't help the addict and cause your own life to be unmanageable. The addict can turn these well-meant actions into an excuse to continue acting out. When spouses realize the futility of their efforts and the amount of time and energy invested in a lost cause, frustration sets in.

Myth #7:
I'm worthless if my spouse doesn't approve of me and accept me.

Reality
Feelings of rejection are normal when you discover your spouse's addiction. However, your self worth is not synonymous with another human being's opinion of you. As a Christian, you are

forgiven and have been brought into an intimate relationship with Christ. Consequently, you are totally accepted by God (Col. 1:21-22). That is your identity. God has placed within you needs that only He can meet.

Many of us marry believing we have found the one magical person who can meet all of our needs. This is not God's idea. As humans we are broken people. We live with the consequences of our own actions and the actions of others. Enjoying the approval of others feels good when we receive it, but we cannot depend on that for our self worth. This dependency on others' approval will keep us chained to a shame-based identity.

In Galatians 1:10, Paul writes: "Am I now trying to win the approval of men, or of God? Or am I trying to please men? If I were still trying to please men, I would not be a servant of Christ." By allowing the addict in your life to determine your feelings about yourself, you give him or her control over you. Many spouses and addicts are affirmationally starved people. We long for the approval of others. Part of working through the rejection is learning to value the constant approval of God over the conditional approval of a spouse or others.

Myth #8:

I'll be a failure if I get a divorce. My spouse will eventually "get it" and stop acting out if I stay no matter what happens.

<u>Reality</u>

Making a commitment to marriage is not equivalent to making a commitment to tolerate abusive behavior or sexual acting out. Staying does not guarantee that the addict will work on changing his or her behavior. Your spouse's abandonment fears preceded your relationship. Your lack of boundaries won't cure his or her fears. Working on your own boundaries and limits will be important to your recovery and will eventually be a blessing to the addict as well.

Reconciliation is a two way street. Divorce doesn't mean you have failed. Toughing it out doesn't mean you are more spiritual. Reconciliation will depend on both you and the addict doing your work. The decisions and choices of others don't make you a failure. The reality is that some addicts choose their addiction over their marriage. Your identity in Christ isn't dependent on what your partner chooses.

Myth #9:

I need to know every detail of what my partner has done for me to be able to trust him or her in the future.

Reality

This belief is another way a spouse can attempt to control the addiction. Honesty is an important element of intimacy. However, real trust will be built on a newly developed sense of connectedness between two whole individuals, not from knowing all of the graphic details of your partner's acting out behaviors. The chapter on disclosure details how disclosure needs to take place.

Trust will come with consistency over time and when the marriage is ultimately surrendered to Christ. Surrendering control over the uncontrollable is part of the key to experiencing freedom and intimacy in marriage.

Myth #10:

Just looking at pornography isn't really adultery.

Reality

One of the Greek words translated adultery in the New Testament is "porneia." Jesus is quoted in Matthew 5 as saying that whoever looks at a woman lustfully has committed adultery with her in his heart. A popular television series ran episodes about a man who was struggling to have sexual intercourse with his wife. She later caught him masturbating to images in pornographic magazines. Rather than insist on fidelity in their marriage, she pasted pictures of her face on the pornographic images in the magazine. This wasn't helpful and her husband was enabled to continue in his destructive behavior. It did nothing to help them have an intimate connection in their marriage.

As a spouse, when you discover your partner's involvement with pornography, the feeling of devastation sets in. It cuts to your soul when you try to compare yourself with airbrushed images and graphic videos. Pornography involves your partner bringing third parties into your sexual relationship. Intercourse with a spouse cannot be the intimate connection God planned if other sexual behavior is regularly a substitute.

Myth #11:
It's not Biblical to abstain from sex with your spouse.

Reality
In 1 Corinthians 7, the Bible gives permission for husband and wife to abstain from sex for a period of time under certain circumstances. Many couples make the decision to have periods of abstinence in their marriage to focus on non-sexual forms of intimacy. Their time apart sexually is used to learn what it means to be present with each other during sex as well as what God desires for them sexually. In addition, a period of abstinence can help reset the addict's brain chemistry that may have been altered because of the addiction.

Sometimes periods of abstinence come naturally due to illness or singleness. God can give you what you need for periods of abstinence. It is a myth that a man or woman cannot stay healthy without acting on sexual energy.

Myth #12:
Obedience to God will keep me from experiencing pain.

Reality
Actually the reverse may be true. God never promises an absence of pain to those who are obedient to Him. In Romans 8, Paul tells us that nothing can separate us from the love of God and that He will cause all things to work together for good if we are seeking His purposes for our lives.

Sometimes people experience intense pain in the midst of a growth spurt. I remember a relative who grew 6 feet tall in junior high. He had to wear knee braces to handle the rapid growth and intense pain. Emotional growth can be painful as well. By definition growth involves a level of discomfort if not outright pain. As you grow through the journey of recovery, there will be moments of discomfort and pain. And then there will be seasons of joy and celebration!

Myth #13:

Only the addict should go to counseling. I don't need help because I didn't act out or cause the problem.

Reality

As a spouse, you have been wounded and perhaps traumatized by the reality of your partner's sexual addiction. And you have issues that affect you. According to one study referenced in the trauma chapter, 81% of spouses were sexually abused as children. There are other types of trauma as well. You will need help as you go through the grieving process.

Myth #14:

Time heals all wounds.

Reality

Time is not an automatic healer. Time alone may actually cause harm rather than healing. If you have a serious accident and are bleeding profusely, time, without some other help, won't heal the wound. In fact, time may bring disability and death. A spouse may stuff feelings. He or she may take on an addiction or continue a pre-existing one to avoid dealing with pain. Another response may be to act like the tough girl or guy and convince oneself that she or he has dealt with it. The spouse may stay on this path for years without dealing with the wounds. Recovery comes from allowing yourself to grieve, facing the pain, and letting God heal.

Myth #15:

Recovery happens when the addict is delivered and the spouse forgives and gets past the hurt.

Reality

God is fully capable of immediately delivering the sex addict from his or her addiction. However, we have not seen it happen that way. Some sex addicts may say that they have immediate delivery and have no need for a recovery program. Usually, those addicts later realize it takes some time and work and decide to become part of a recovery program. Addiction is a process and so is transformation. It requires time and effort.

The process of forgiveness is an essential part of the spouse's recovery. You may be tempted to quickly say, "I forgive you," to ease the tension in yourself and in the sex addict. Don't take the process of forgiveness lightly. Grieving comes before forgiveness. One needs to acknowledge the losses and hurts and not skip over the process too quickly. In addition, forgiveness may involve dealing with other past betrayals that you as a spouse need to address.

Conclusion

There is a recovery saying that goes, "The truth will set you free, but first it will make you mad." As a spouse you will be facing truth that you never imagined you would when you said, "I do." Facing truth is a process you will go through on this journey. You will experience grief, anger, sadness, pain, hope, healing, and joy (not necessarily in that order). Healing isn't a linear process that is done by completing a checklist. Healing the wounds that sexual addiction inflicts involves facing the wounds directly. Hope and healing do come. Others in recovery will help you along the way. You are building a wall of recovery. Don't let the myths deprive you of life-giving healing.

Chapter Seven

To Tell Or Not To Tell:
The Disclosure Dilemma

D isclosure to the spouse is one of the most controversial aspects of recovery. Yet, dealing with this topic is critical in the healing journey. As a spouse, listening to the addict in your life share how they have violated the marriage covenant will be one of the most painful things you ever endure.

Sexual integrity issues are discovered in marriages in a variety of ways. Perhaps you stumbled upon credit card receipts, phone bills, or overheard a phone call. It may be that you had a hunch and went looking for proof. (I often tell spouses that they have become so good at checking into a partner's past that they may be developing careers as private investigators.) Or you might have discovered it due to a guilty conscience. Perhaps the addict in your life simply couldn't carry the burden anymore and confessed his problem with sexual integrity.

Regardless of how you found out, it was one of the most shocking, devastating, and painful things you have ever discovered. The pain of betrayal strikes at the core of your being. Questions begin to race through your mind. Why wasn't I enough? Has he/she told me everything? What if this gets worse? Will I have to go through this again? Would he have gone outside of the marriage if I'd looked better, done my hair differently, weighed less, or had plastic surgery?

The moment of disclosure/discovery of your spouse's sexual addiction places the two of you at radically different places. Beginning the process of recovery takes the couple through a journey of conflict, confusion, and chaos. It's difficult for a couple to navigate, and professional help is almost always required.

The addict's world	The spouses world
The secret is out. I don't have to live a double life anymore	I've never felt so much pain and devastation In my life
I'm growing spiritually and becoming a man of integrity	I've been betrayed
I've never loved my wife more than I do right now	I've never felt less loved, valued, or safe
I now realize how valuable the gift of my marriage really is	I never realized how little our marriage relationship meant to him
I'm finally becoming an honest man	How could he have lied to me for so long?
I understand the healing process will take 3-5 years. I think I can speed it up because I want it with all of my heart.	Three years seems like eternity with this level of pain. I don't know if I can take it.
I love my men's group. I finally have support and accountability in my life. I have friends who understand.	I wonder how many people know about us. Will they think I'm married to some kind of a pervert?

As soon as sexual sin is discovered, you will experience a variety of emotions. The response is typically shock or anger. As a therapist, I have been involved in more disclosure sessions than I can remember. There is almost always disclosure at some level before this session takes place. By the time the couple comes to a disclosure session, there has already been some level of information shared. It may be nothing more than the original discovery of the sexual acting out. At this point, it is normal to experience the feelings discussed in chapter 2 & 3 of this book. Things like shock, anger, anxiety, and depression are normal when you discover that your husband/wife has committed sexual sin in the marriage.

Experiencing the consequences of another's sin is a hard concept to grasp. Theologically and emotionally, it is difficult to explain. The reality is that in this world, we live with the consequences of the actions of others on a daily basis. You may think, "I've thrown myself into this marriage and given 110%. How could this happen to me? I've done everything I could possibly do. Why is God letting me down?" Sexual sin in a marriage will challenge your view of God. You might even find yourself questioning his existence. Again, it is normal to experience these emotions and questions. Don't beat yourself up or think that you're unfaithful to God because you are experiencing feelings and raising questions.

At this point, a Christian spouse may find comfort in the Psalms. A common form of literature in the western world in Old Testament times was called lament. Many of the writings in Job, Jeremiah, Lamentations, as well as the Psalms follow this form. Lament is the predominant form of literature found in the book of Psalms.[35] A large volume of writing in these books is devoted to people expressing their frustration, hurt, despair, and even anger towards God. These were people who lived when their lives and faith were threatened. They knew the cruelty and lack of justice in their communities. The writings of David in Psalm 32 and 51 reveal that he intimately knew the frustration and pain of experiencing marital unfaithfulness. People knew what it was like to experience the consequences of another's sins. At times they cried out as individuals and as communities for God to take drastic action and punish those who caused their pain. The people had no problem expressing to God the depths of their pain. When you discover that sexual sin has entered your marriage, the emotions are similar to what people expressed throughout the Psalms. Odds are that even in the worst moments of your pain you have never expressed some of the things that the Psalmist shares.

Rest assured that God can handle your emotions. It won't feel like it at times, but he can take whatever you need to express. One of my favorite stories is about the late Elizabeth Kubler Ross. In the 1940's she was training chaplains to help terminally ill people and their family members, in a Chicago area hospital. The chaplains were becoming frustrated with terminally ill people and their families who were angry at God. Ms. Ross simply looked at them and told them that "God was big enough to take it."[36] God is big enough to take whatever feelings you may need to express. He already knows them anyway. It is much more therapeutic to be honest and express these feelings than to deny them and suffer in silence.

Do I Really Need To Know And How Will It Affect Me?

Sexual integrity issues result from issues with intimacy. The ultimate purpose of disclosure is to be able to participate in the healing process, and build genuinely intimate relationships. We believe that disclosure is necessary in order to experience genuine connection in marriage.

Ask yourself what information do you need in order to move forward? Do you want details to confirm your fears? Then we suggest that once your suspicions have been validated, you have enough detail to move forward. Having all the gory details may add more material that will cause you pain that you don't need in order to heal.

There are different approaches to disclosure of sexual acting out in a relationship. Over the years, I have worked with people who have experienced each of these different approaches. Pastors and counselors alike differ on this issue. Some believe in no disclosure and others in full disclosure with graphic detail. As a spouse, you may go through periods where you feel like knowing everything. At other times, you may wish you knew nothing. While initially painful, 93% of spouses are glad they went through disclosure[37].

One school of thought says that there should be no disclosure. This may be based on the idea that "what you don't know won't hurt you." Or it may come from the application of the 9th step in the twelve-step programs. This step reads, "Made direct amends to such people wherever possible, except when to do so would injure them or others."[38] Carol Ross, a nationally known expert in the field, calls this the "ninth step slide." This is based upon the idea that a spouse would be harmed if they knew what the addict had done. I would ask, has the harm come from the fact that a spouse is being told the truth, or is the harm coming from the fact that the addict has sexually acted out? This approach is dangerous for an addict. Another Alcoholics Anonymous saying is, "You are only as sick as your secrets."[39] Secrecy is the gasoline that fuels the engine of an addiction. The more secrets an addict tries to keep, the more likely he/she is to act out.

Another approach to disclosure suggests that the addict present information in small amounts to the spouse. Not surprisingly, this approach is usually the idea of the addict. It may be their way of only admitting to what they get caught doing. This approach may appear to make disclosure easier for the addict; but it's the most painful approach to take to the spouse. Many years ago, I went to an oral surgeon who told me I had a wisdom tooth that was going bad. He suggested that we remove all four of them at the same time. The reason was that the pain and recovery time would be the same. I could go through the experience four times or I could go through it once. I was quickly convinced that I would be much better off if this was a onetime event. Disclosure works the same way. It can come out in one painful, messy operation, or the pain can be experienced over and over again. For this reason, it is critical that the addict be well-prepared at the time of the disclosure session.

Another problem with disclosing in small amounts is that it empowers the addict and places the spouse at his/her mercy. It assumes that the addict is capable of knowing what the spouse can and cannot handle. In reality, it's the addict's way of hanging onto the addiction. The attitudes needed for a disclosure to be effective are contradicted by this approach. Disclosure is difficult for both spouses and addicts. The needs of the spouse at this stage of the journey are critical.

While initially painful, 93% of spouses are glad they went through disclosure

An extreme approach is full disclosure with graphic detail. I recently had a man want to disclose to his wife in this way. The imagery it would have placed in her mind would have been horrific. We worked on how he could present this information without making it even more difficult for his wife. As stated earlier, there are times when you will feel like knowing every detail of the sexual sin. Ask yourself what is happening with you at the times you feel the need for this information. Are you down on yourself? Are you feeling the need to punish the addict in your life? Are you looking for a reason to be angry? Are you comparing yourself to airbrushed images of women in pornographic material? Chances are you are experiencing the low self-esteem that comes with being violated. It may be that the mental measuring stick has come out and you are trying to decide whether or not you measure up. Punishment may feel tempting at times. You have probably had a number of fantasies about what you would like to do to the person who has offended you. I've had spouses present many creative ideas. Or it may be that you are experiencing some feelings *about* having feelings of anger. Some Christians have been taught that they should not feel anger. When they experience anger, they begin to feel guilty about having the feeling. You don't need to justify your feelings, especially about being sexually betrayed. Your feelings are yours. They aren't right or wrong. What we do with them gets into the realm of morality. Most parents can relate to the feeling of wanting to wring their children's necks. It is okay for them to feel. It is NOT okay for them to act upon these feelings. Denial of feelings will breed silent obsession. Pretending that they don't exist will make you obsess more about the problem, and is much more likely to lead to an unhealthy response than honesty about the feelings.

The approach we recommend is that there be a full disclosure without graphic detail. In almost 25 years of working with churches and as a professional counselor, I have found that this is the approach that works best for long term recovery and for healing the marriage.

Sexual imagery is powerful. The imprinting upon the brain has long lasting effects. People can remember the details of their first exposure to pornography, though this experience may have been decades old. Yet they typically won't remember what was seen two days ago on the evening news. There are a number of neurochemical factors involved, but for the purpose of this discussion you do not want graphic details being disclosed. If I tell you I have a cat, you will form your own safe image of what that cat will look like. If I tell you I have a cat that has grey hair with white spots and has a hot temper, you develop a different image. When a sex addict discloses the graphic details of a sex act or explicit details of a human body, the spouse may be left with graphic imagery that they don't wish to have.

A sex addict can disclose to his/her spouse that they have a problem with Internet pornography and be completely honest. They don't have to disclose which web site they went to and what the imagery they were watching involved. An addict can disclose that they have had multiple affairs, without giving physical details of the affair partner or the acts they performed. In this way, they can be honest without creating more misery than necessary for the spouse. They may need to have additional conversations with mentors, sponsors and accountability partners. But the spouse does not benefit from these details.

What Do I Need To Know?

What should you expect to hear from your partner during disclosure? There is information you need to have in order to make decisions about your own self-care. You need to know whether or not your partner has been physically involved with an affair partner. If so, you will need to be tested for sexually transmitted diseases. And there may be a period of time where you need to remain abstinent from a sexual relationship with your partner.

Another issue is pornography. Is the acting out limited to pornography? Was it accessed via a home computer and is there the possibility that your children may have been exposed? I recently counseled a nine-year old female sex addict. This young lady had discovered her father's Internet pornography. Instead of telling her mother, she became addicted and acted out for over 9 months. It is important that the needs of your children be addressed in the event that they have been exposed. With the average age of first exposure to pornography for a male being age 5, (age 8 in surveys of males and females) this becomes a critical issue.[40] (See appendix C for more information on the impact of pornography on children and families.)

Is the acting out heterosexual or does it involve same-sex activity? If an affair has taken place, is it with someone that you know? If so, you have the right to decide how you want to handle that relationship. If your partner had an affair with a close friend or someone you work with, you may need to deal with that relationship for your own self-care.

Another issue may involve money. I always encourage sexual addicts to disclose the amount of money that has been spent on the addiction. They also need to disclose how they covered up the expenditures. Was the job loss because of downsizing, or was their a termination due to sexual acting out on work time? Seventy percent of Internet pornography is viewed between the hours of 9:00 am and 5:00 pm. People are losing jobs due to inappropriate sexual activity on the Internet. It is rare that we ever conduct groups that don't have at least one individual who has just lost a long career due to sexual acting out on company time.

Perhaps there are cell phones, email addresses, and other forms of keeping in touch with an affair partner that need to be revealed. If the addict has incurred debts while acting out, this needs to be revealed. These methods of communication need to be terminated immediately. Contact with affair partners needs to end immediately. It takes less than 30 seconds to pick up a phone in the presence of accountability and terminate all contact with an affair partner. The feelings and relationship with the spouse are much more important than those of an affair partner. If the marriage is to become the center of your family, all contact with affair partners must come to an abrupt end.

Rules For Disclosure Sessions (a note to therapists)

Preparation for the session is critical. The therapist needs to meet with the spouse and the addict prior to the disclosure session and explain what will be happening. The individual disclosing sexual acting out will write out what they want to say and how it will be expressed. Graphic details will be eliminated. Be aware of tendencies to rationalize and justify any actions. Eliminate any requests for forgiveness. This can make a spouse feel like she has to make a decision to forgive on the spot. Forgiveness is a process that doesn't come quickly. The disclosure to the spouse must involve the presentation of brokenness and humility, if the marriage is to be improved. Statements like, "I'm sorry, but I was having a hard time at work when I acted out," or "I feel awful about what I've done, but you weren't being very supportive at the time," are examples of statements that reflect defensiveness and justification for one's actions. A man or woman who is genuinely in recovery will begin to reflect a spirit of brokenness and humility without rationalization. He/she will also need to learn to validate your pain and develop empathy for you. Your emotions and hurt cannot be minimized by either of you.

Evaluate the addict's motivation. Does the addict want to disclose to heal the marriage? Is he disclosing to clear his conscience? Look at the level of anger. Some addicts have wanted to disclose graphic details to hurt the spouse. Disclosure is a therapeutic process designed to build intimacy in a relationship. Does the couple desire reconciliation and healing? Carefully evaluate the purpose of the disclosure session.

Consider the spouses needs as you prepare for this session. The spouse may choose to drive to this session in a separate car or have a friend bring her (though they would not participate in the session). If there are children, it is best that you not leave this session and immediately pick them up from school. Do not plan on a disclosure session right before family members are coming for an extended visit. Make sure people in your support system are notified that you will be experiencing a difficult session, and don't hesitate to use them. Hopefully the spouse will have made contact with people who have walked this road before. They can be supportive and take the journey with you.

Disclosure sessions need to take place in the presence of a therapist or pastor who is specifically trained in dealing with sexual integrity issues. A minimum of 2 hours needs to be allowed for this session. A session might begin with a brief feelings check. The sexual addict will share his statement with the spouse. The spouse needs to have freedom to express whatever feelings come up and to ask any questions. The addict needs to be willing to share anything that the spouse needs to hear. The therapist may need to intervene at this point and help the spouse determine if the answer to the question would do more harm than good (i.e. graphic details). Depending on where the recovery process is at the time of the session, the grieving process will either begin or move to a new level. The spouse will enter a time of disorientation, confusion, and mixed emotions. Safety arrangements must be made. A spouse may need a medical evaluation at some point in the process. The session needs to end with each spouse affirming their commitment to personal healing. The addict needs to take responsibility for his/her actions, and present their plan for how they will manage their sexual integrity issues. As a spouse, you will need to make the same commitment to healing. At the time of a disclosure session, you will probably not be able to articulate a specific plan. That's ok. At this point your job is to grieve the losses you are experiencing. Your therapist will work with you on specific plans at a later date. For now, it is important that you commit to the journey of healing. At this point, you are making that commitment for yourself. Regardless of what the addict in your life is doing, you need to heal your own wounds. Even if the addict chooses not to get sober, you still have been wounded and need to go through the process.

Disclosure On The Part Of The Spouse

In earlier chapters, this book talks about getting in touch with your coping skills as a spouse. Through the years, I have seen spouses cope with the stress and pressure in their marriage with everything from overeating and compulsive spending, to chronic raging and initiating a revenge affair. In our pain, we often get desperate for relief. It is easy to seek false solutions when we feel desperate. Or perhaps you have been emotionally dishonest with your mate. Have you told him/her that things were okay when in reality you were hurting? Many spouses have been guilty of emotional dishonesty. Have you run up credit cards that your partner is unaware of? At some point, you may need to disclose some of these issues to your partner. In no way does this put blame on you for the actions of your partner. You are not responsible for them. You are responsible only for how *you* choose to react and cope with the devastating pain. Part of the journey will be learning healthier coping strategies.

In no way does this put blame on you for the actions of your partner. You are not responsible for them. You are responsible only for how *you* choose to react and cope.

Honesty is foundational for healing intimacy issues. This will require an effort on the part of the husband and the wife. Recovery in marriage involves honesty on the part of everyone. It may be that as a spouse you need to make amends with your children. Perhaps they have been neglected during the insanity. It may be that while being emotionally shut down from your partner, you took your anger out on your children. Disclosure is like surgery. Cutting out the infection is painful and will require a long period of recovery. It is also part of the road to healing.

Rebuilding Intimacy

As you journey through the crisis, it will be hard to imagine that the painful disclosure session may become one of the foundational acts of intimacy in your marriage. Like surgery, you would never volunteer to go through it again. Yet it may be something you look back on, as a time when you and your partner became completely honest with one another for the first time.

Intimacy can be a tough word to define. As you are beginning this journey, make a commitment to not define intimacy as sex. Nonsexual intimacy is a key to a great sex life anyway. First things first. One of the best definitions I ever heard of intimacy came from a young man who was 16 years old. When asked to define intimacy, he said that it was "the ability of two people to be real with each other." My favorite definition of intimacy was based on the work of Claudia Black. This was given to me by a man in one of our couples groups at Faithful and True Atlanta.

"Intimacy is when I give the other the very weapons of my destruction (in my case the knowledge of and truth about me.) Then, after taking the risk to share, the other uses the weapons of my destruction – not to destroy me, but to defend me."

This involves being real on a mental, emotional, and spiritual level. Depending on your family of origin baggage, you may struggle more in one of these areas than others. Intimacy involves connection at multiple levels.

Jesus gives a description of intimacy with God that we as his children can imitate. In Mark 12, Jesus is talking to teachers of the law (who probably had intimacy issues themselves).[41] In a typical intimacy avoidance game of one-upmanship, they ask Jesus which is the greatest commandment. The answer he gives is probably not what they expect. He begins by reminding them of the unity of God. "Hear, O Israel, the Lord our God, the Lord is one." (v. 29) The oneness of Father, Son, and Holy Spirit are clearly seen in this text. They have a unity that far exceeds the one flesh union that we strive for in marriage. And their union has not been violated. In looking for a role model for intimacy, do we seek to imitate imperfect people who have intimacy struggles, or do we look to the God who has perfected intimate relationship? Jesus then presents a holistic look at people and the concept of oneness. He tells them to love God with all of their heart (emotions), soul (spirituality), mind (mental processes), and strength (physical being). This might be a way of describing the perfect oneness and unity of God. Please don't get distracted into theological arguments about this text. We miss the point in the process. Jesus gives us a model for balanced, healthy relationships. As the connections grow on all four of these levels, intimacy will develop in your relationship with God and with others. Look at all four of these areas in your life. Take time and make a list of things you can do to help yourself continue to develop emotionally, physically, mentally, and spiritually.

Share your list with a mentor, sponsor, or accountability partner. You may even choose to share it with your marriage partner whenever you feel comfortable. Use this as a tool to share your journey with someone else. You will find that many positive connections and relationships can develop along the way.

Chapter Eight

Boundaries:
Setting Them And Keeping Them

"I keep trying to set boundaries with my husband, but he keeps breaking them and I feel like there is no point in trying."

"I know I need to set limits, but whenever I do I don't enforce them and I end up feeling more helpless than ever."

"I feel like I get run over by everyone. The word 'doormat' must be tattooed across my forehead."

These are the words of some spouses who have begun looking at their boundary issues.

In the early 1970's my family moved into the house where I would spend most of my growing up years. We had a large back yard that was the envy of many kids on the block. One of the first things that dad built was a fence. One of the reasons it went up was to set a boundary. The purpose was to create some safety. It designated a safe area in which my brother, sister, and I could play. It had at least three gates. We weren't trying to avoid our neighbors with the fence. There were ways to come and go when it was appropriate and safe.

Relationships have emotional boundaries. In this chapter we will look at healthy boundaries and differentiate them from unhealthy boundaries.

When I was struggling with religious addiction and codependency issues, my therapist said something to me that resonates to this day. My therapist looked at me and said, "Richard, you don't know where you end and the church begins." This is referred to as enmeshment. Enmeshed relationships appeal to some on the surface. At first an enmeshed relationship may feel close. But eventually people crave space and individuality. The enmeshed relationship will begin to breed resentment.

Have you ever watched professional ice skating? Think of the graceful moves of the skaters as they move to the rhythm of the music. What would happen if someone tied a chain around the two skaters? It would severely restrict their ability to move, and destroy the gracefulness of their skating. Restricting one's individuality within the marriage can look emotionally like the skaters do with the chain. Eventually people try to break free of the chains. And when they do, both people get hurt. Spouses of sex addicts will initially struggle with defining and setting boundaries. Once defined, enforcing them is the next step. This will create anxiety for you initially, but with practice it can become less stressful ... and then begin to feel worth it.

Chapter three looked at different forms of trauma. The type of trauma you experienced will impact the development of boundary issues in relationships. Physical, emotional, spiritual, and sexual abuse will create boundary issues. If invasive forms of trauma are the norm in your family, chances are you will develop loose boundaries. Wounds of abandonment will lead to boundaries that are rigid.

The goal isn't to change someone else. It is to keep yourself safe and focused on healing your own wounds.

Think of the child who grows into adult years unprotected from harm. There will be developmental needs that are unmet. The lack of protection creates an environment where abuse is the norm. Growing up without completing appropriate developmental stages will lead to boundary problems in adult relationships. Spouses often don't trust themselves and deny gut instincts that something is wrong in the marriage. This results from boundary issues in the family of origin. Other trauma may have been been minimized or denied. This will lead to a disconnection with your true self. Many spouses find themselves second-guessing their natural instincts. When we look back throughout the marriage, we typically find that there were clues all along that the spouse missed due to second guessing and denial.

Setting limits can be difficult when you haven't been taught to set them. When you develop the resolve and courage to set limits, maintaining them creates deeper challenges. Addicts will resist your boundaries. Resistance doesn't mean that your boundaries are wrong. It means that your decision to change something in your life may lead to people close to you having to make adjustments. The goal, however, isn't to change someone else. It is to keep yourself safe and focused on healing your own wounds. For example, a spouse who is used to covering up for her husband's acting out by lying to people about his whereabouts may decide to stop for her own sake. The addict will become angry because he could be exposed. The anger of the addict doesn't make the spouse wrong for setting this boundary.

"I remember when I first told my husband that I wouldn't have sex with him until he was tested for sexually transmitted diseases. He was so angry and felt I was trying to punish him. He called me names and said that I had no right to make demands of him. In the past, I would've believed him and given in. When the test came back positive for gonorrhea, I was glad I had enforced this boundary."

When a spouse sets boundaries there will be resistance. Remember, you are setting limits to protect yourself, not manipulate the addict. It is more important that you take care of and respect yourself than to avoid resistance from the addict.

A person with vague limits will take on other's responsibilities without reservation. Healthy relationships have interdependence where both partners give and receive. Relationships without boundaries involve one-way intimacy. One person does most of the giving and ends up quietly resentful.

A good friend and colleague, David Blackwell, introduced me to a life-changing form of therapy. One summer afternoon he invited me to join a small group of people who were working on boundary issues in relationships. Our group didn't meet in an air-conditioned office of a nicely furnished counseling center. Instead, we met in a round pen next to a lake with four-legged therapists – horses. Yes, I can see the skeptical look on your face as you read these words. On that day, I learned just how boundariless I was. I feared rejection if I said "no" to people. Needless to say, I got severely hurt in many relationships. Animals can be great teachers. The use of animals in therapy has been well documented for years. Working with the horses in a therapeutic workshop created an experience for groups that couldn't be replicated in talk therapy. Many treatment centers in the western United States use equine assisted therapy.

Through the years, David introduced me to a book by Linda Kohanov entitled, *The Tao of Equus*. Linda makes a number of therapeutic observations about working with horses that mirror the experience of spouses. I'm sure that at times on this journey you will feel like referring to your husband as a certain part of a horse's anatomy. Another article I received was written by Diane Lindig Tobin. She presents some lessons that can be learned in working with horses that are applicable to spouses of sexual addicts. The quotes below are taken from her article[42].

- Horses:
  You must treat your horse not like an object to be pulled around on, but like a dance partner.

  > With Spouses: Marriages and dance floors can bring pleasant experiences, but if your partner is constantly pushed around, they will eventually begin to resist. After being pushed and pulled in unnatural ways, the experience becomes painful.

- Horses: *Stay present.*

  > With Spouses: Addicts retreat into fantasy to avoid reality. Spouses may be retreating into idealistic relational fantasies to avoid pain. One of Virginia Satir's favorite ways

to begin a sentence was, "at this moment in time." Living in the present can be a challenge when fantasy is a primary coping skill.

• Horses:
There is never a time when you are interacting with your horse that disrespect is acceptable.

With Spouses: Respect is one of the top intimacy needs most people desire. Without respect, the horse will not move towards you in the relationship. In the same way, marriages without respect will result in stalemates.

• Horses:
Be absolutely consistent with your horse in what is acceptable or not acceptable behavior.

With Spouses: Strive to set consistent boundaries and consistently follow them up with consequences if they are not honored. Create accountability within your support system. You may even want to create consequences for yourself for not following through with your limits.

• Horses:
Sweat the small stuff. Remember body language, position, eye contact etc. are strong signals to them.

With Spouses: Nonverbals are important. If there is a discrepancy between what someone says and what they do, resolve it in favor of what they do. I tell spouses to listen with their eyes. Believe what you see. I remember at an equine therapy session, one of the spouses was trying to get a horse to come to her. She shook her hand and made a stomping motion towards the horse while saying "come here." The horse didn't listen to her words. The horse listened to the threatening body language. When you are trying to set a boundary with the addict, make sure you sweat the small stuff. Make your words consistent with your tone of voice and body language.

Learning to trust your intuition as a spouse is a difficult process. Family rules may have taught you to deny and minimize your feelings. The addict in your life has probably taught you to second-guess yourself. Addicts are good at getting spouses to deny their own reality. Part of the journey of recovery is learning to trust your instincts.

Poor boundaries will typically lead a spouse to try to work the addict's program for him. The illusion of control creates a temporary feeling of safety. It's the belief that if I manage his recovery and keep tabs on everything he does, I will somehow be safe. However, the key to freedom is not in trying to control. Freedom is found in release - one of the most difficult things you will do as a spouse. Once you give up trying to control the impossible, you will experience a sense of relief from a huge burden. Ultimately, the addict is the only one who can save himself from the path of destruction. Releasing the addict to experience the full consequences of his behavior may be his only hope for recovery. Ask yourself if what you are doing is genuinely helping the addict. Are your actions preventing him from experiencing consequences? If so, you may be creating more of an emotional struggle for yourself later on. Perhaps you are the parent of a teenager who repeatedly gets tickets for driving under the influence of alcohol. If you continually bail the child out of jail, what will he learn? Rescuing him won't help him grow up. He needs to experience consequences. Otherwise, he will learn that there are no consequences and that mom and dad will always be there to bail him out. Giving up the rescue fantasies are difficult. However, there is a difference between giving and enabling. Learn to tell the difference by seeing if your giving is helping the addict get better or worse.

Equine-assisted therapy begins by entering the round pen, looking at the horses, and choosing which one you want to work with. Consider this story from equine assisted therapy. Linda Kohanov presents this case study which has application to spouses.

Hawk, a new addition to the herd, strained his neck as far as possible over the fence and nibbled at Joy's coat. "This one is so cute," she said, giggling with delight. Joy had picked a bully in a state of dysfunction, somewhat like the descriptions of the men in her life. Linda wanted to see if Joy could recognize the danger he represented. Joy had read Hawk as "very sweet, highly affectionate, and outgoing. We had an instant connection," she said excitedly, "like I already know him. I feel the safest with Hawk." Linda said, "Before you make your final decision, let's see how the horses react when there's something important at stake." Linda tossed a single flake of alfalfa into the center of the paddock, and all the horses headed toward it. Rasa managed to grab a mouthful before Hawk reared up, swooped down, and tried to bite her on the flank. He viciously kicked at Noche and chased Comet halfway around the corral. Joy gasped, "Oh my God, I do know that guy. He's like most of the people in my life." Joy had mistakenly associated the feeling of familiarity with safety. She had misread Hawk's disrespect of boundaries as affection. When he nibbled her coat, he was trying to see how much Joy would let him get away with, how easily she could be dominated. Joy had a tendency to be captivated by superficially outgoing personalities. Linda, pointed out a healthier horse, Rasa, to Joy and showed her how Rasa didn't play games with Hawk, but walked away and ignored Hawk when he was being aggressive. Rasa modeled healthy boundaries. Possessing neither the skills nor the resources to make it on her own, young Joy found ways to avoid neglect or abandonment, an especially important consideration since her father was an alcoholic and her mother was a raging narcissist. Joy's grandmother, the powerful matriarch of the family, fortified her regal position by controlling the wealth and social standing of the family (everyone else stood to benefit from,). She doled out fleeting approval to those who indulged her whims while enduring her cruel insults and erratic, manipulative behavior. Joy's sympathetic demeanor and high tolerance for abuse raised her to the status of favored grandchild. She tried to please at all cost, making sure the people in power needed her in some way; or at the very least found her cute, humble, and ingratiating enough to want her around.[43]

There are several things in Joy's story that reveal boundary issues in relationships. She would make commitments and read too much into relationships based on only brief first impressions. Some might say "love at first sight." One recovering spouse shared that he could walk into any Sunday school class full of singles and instantly pick one that would ruin his life. He was married to a female sex addict for 15 years. He once said to me, "My picker is broken." Joy's choice of a horse was much like the choices she made with men. This is why it is so important for you as a spouse to take your own journey of recovery. Otherwise, you will probably find yourself in another relationship with a sex addict, alcoholic, drug addict, or batterer.

Most married people know that moment of startling realization when they discover that their partner has faults that they had missed during dating. Maybe the addict in your life started out sweet, loving, and gentle. But when something important was at stake, he may have reverted back to addictive behaviors.

Like many spouses, Joy had a high tolerance for pain. She was conditioned to be this way by her grandmother. She became attracted to men who would harm her. "Those who betray read their victims well. They appeal to the emptiness, the unfinished business, and the wounds of others. The promise is designed to fix, to heal, to resolve or to make up for what has happened. The promise is so appealing that intuitions are set aside."[44] The illusion of safety becomes so powerful that caution is thrown to the wind. Then when reality sets in, the shame is overwhelming. Joy was trying to heal her wounds by repeating what she knew to do. We are creatures of habit. Until we learn to do something different, we will continue in the same cycle of destructive relationships. One of my favorite therapy sayings is, "if you always do what you always did, you always get what you always got."

If Virginia Satir were alive today, I'm convinced she would be a best friend to people in recovery from sexual addiction and their families. Virginia, in her change model, talks about how people are creatures of habit until the introduction of a "foreign element."[45] This can be a new piece of information, a glimmer of hope, seeing someone model a different way of life, or simply trying something different. Once this happens, you can begin breaking the cycle. Unfortunately, we often have to get deeply wounded before we begin seeking something new. Yet while breaking the cycle of familiarity is difficult, the results are life changing.

Admittedly, healthy people can be boring at times. There may not be an adrenaline rush and you won't see shooting stars during the first kiss. However, life won't be boring forever. As intimacy grows and develops, new types of excitement beyond your wildest dreams can be possible.

During this time of transition, you will need the support of your recovery family. The addict who is resisting your new boundaries may not be capable of giving support for your recovery. That's ok. He needs to be taking his own journey of healing. Your recovery family will be able to provide you with the love and support you need as you make these changes.

One obstacle you may face is that historically the church has supported and honored people who don't have good boundaries. You may have been called "the person who never says no." Or you may be known as the person who does everything. People who don't have limits get taken advantage of in relationships. The church won't fall apart if you can't teach class year round and cook for every dinner.

Setting boundaries and enforcing them will be life-giving once you become accustomed to a new lifestyle. I remember one night at the counseling center a female addict came over in front of my family and wanted to hug me. I held both of my hands up in the air as a gesture to say stop. I instantly told her that I don't hug female addicts who are new to our groups out of respect to my wife and family. She was disappointed, but accepted my boundary. Nine months later, she found out *from her group leader* that a lesson she needed to learn and begin to look at was how she had lived without boundaries as a lifestyle.

In chapter 2 I shared how my issues had led me to attract women who would hurt me. Like Joy, I fell for the horse that appeared to be warm and charming. Shame would keep me in friendships in which I did all of the giving. They were one way relationships. I've been described as being loyal to a fault. It's true. I've been incredibly loyal to people who love taking advantage of my lack of boundaries. Part of the journey for me has been learning to say no. I've also had to learn to wade into relationships and discover who I'm with, instead of diving into seemingly calm waters with a strong undertow.

I remember the first time I went to a group for codependency. It was a class through a community education program at Emory University. The group leader asked us to go for a week and not do anything for anyone. Our Bible study group at church was talking about being servants. I thought I was going to go insane during that week. The level of inactivity and inability to rescue people made me feel like I was losing my mind. It was one of the best things that could've happened. I learned that the world wouldn't fall apart if I wasn't there to take care of everything. And things at church could function just fine without me teaching and trying to take care of everyone. I needed to redefine myself in relationship to the church and to other people. Part of that journey has meant severing some relationships, especially with destructive women. It's meant setting appropriate boundaries in all relationships.

To set relationship boundaries is to risk losing the love you've craved for a very long time. To start saying "no" to controlling people is scary. The belief behind lack of boundaries is the fear of loss. I feared that I would lose relationships and lose significance if I said "no" to people. Perhaps you have fears of losing financial resources, or you might fear the anger of the addict. As I'm writing this, the movie "What's love got to do with it" is playing on TV. In the Ike and Tina Turner story, Tina is coping with being a mother in a relationship where her husband Ike is regularly beating her physically and emotionally. Tina says "yes" to Ike for fear of losing her life. Breaking free may require some steps to insure your safety. Taking care of yourself may feel scary at first, simply because it is new. As you develop new attitudes and beliefs about yourself and feel stronger, you will discover that letting go of control is the way to serenity.

Overcoming Barriers: A Boundaries Lifestyle

One of the cultural traps that can hinder establishing good boundaries is giving reasons for every decision.[46] This makes it hard to communicate clear limits. Rather than accepting your "no" the addict will start critiquing your reasons or reorganizing your life. You might hear lines like, "Well, if you would organize your time this way, then you could do what I want us to do." Or it might be, "If I was important to you then you would do _____." Rather than honoring your boundary, there is an attempt to manipulate.

One of the things I've had to learn is that not every "no" is about personal rejection. I'm blessed to work with a wonderful staff at Faithful and True Marriages. Not only are these people coworkers, they are some of my best friends. Sometimes they have to say "no" to me. It's not about rejection. It's about their need for self-care. Sometimes they say "yes" and other times they don't. If I'm feeling hurt or have questions, I have the freedom to talk about these feelings and ask questions. We have all learned as a staff to honor and validate feelings without necessarily changing a decision.

The Guilt Trap

Addicts are notorious for using guilt trips to project responsibility for their decisions onto their spouses. You probably know the gut-wrenching feeling when you've been manipulated into agreeing to do something you don't want to do. Boundary crashers will convince you that if you don't do it their way, they will die and it will be your entire fault. "Sherry, if you leave, the kids will be devastated and will hate you forever. I could lose my job." This is what one addict recently said to his spouse as a way to get her to stay. He was a pastor at a church and believed he would lose his job if his wife left him. He used guilt to manipulate Sherry (not her real name). Guilt won't solve problems. It delays difficult decisions and typically makes the outcome worse. Remember, resistance to your boundaries doesn't make you wrong for setting them. Boundaries are not meant to punish people. They are created for your safety. The boundaries you set need to be well thought out so that you can enforce them. Feelings of vindictiveness and a desire to punish the person who betrayed you are normal. Anger is a part of grieving. However, making life-changing decisions while you are feeling like taking revenge is not wise. It will come back to bite you. Use your recovery family to keep you accountable for your attitudes when setting boundaries.

Using Boundaries To Isolate Yourself

Boundaries protect, but they shouldn't isolate you from contact with people. Removing yourself from a situation when you are unsafe is appropriate. Trusting blindly is not appropriate. Throwing yourself wide open emotionally to someone who has betrayed you is foolish. Boundaries need to be for your personal safety, not controlling the addict. Ask yourself if you are withdrawing for safety or revenge. Reconciliation and rebuilding trust is the goal. These goals can't be accomplished if you are completely walled off from people or if you are trying to hurt them. Of course, the process of reconciliation and rebuilding trust will take time. Let the process evolve in God's time. Take your journey without forcing yourself to operate on the addict's timetable.

All Or Nothing Thinking

One thing that makes it difficult for some spouses to enforce boundaries is the belief that there are only two options: tolerate the status quo or get a divorce. Either option feels hopeless when you are beginning this journey. Boundaries aren't all or nothing. One of the many bright spouses I've been blessed to work with told me how she learned this lesson. Jeannie shared about how her husband arrogantly told her she was just going to have to tolerate slips because they were a part of the disease. Jeannie rightly confronted him on his attitude and surprised him with the way she communicated her limits. She said to him, "If you have a slip with pornography, I will be hurt deeply but it won't be a deal breaker. But if you have sex with someone other than me, the kids and I are off to Indiana." Notice she didn't say that she was divorcing him. She knew better than to make a life changing decision at a time when there would be such intense emotion. She said she would detach from him to make some decisions. Since that time, her husband has communicated how grateful he was that she confronted him and set this boundary. It blessed his recovery as well as hers. That was six years ago. Today, Matt and Jeannie are doing extremely well. They are breaking the cycle in their family and their children will have a different legacy.

Examples Of Boundaries

As writers, we surveyed our clients and asked them to share some of the boundaries that they have found helpful in their recovery. These are some of the most common ones we saw. We are also listing some of the most common ways that spouses crash boundaries along with some comments. Remember, you will need to explore your own boundaries as part of your journey of healing.

1. *My spouse must be in a recovery program for sexual addiction or we will not have sex. The bedroom needs to be "undefiled."* Communicate to the addict that you are not willing to share him/her sexually with anyone else.

2. *If my husband is mentally undressing someone else when we are in a restaurant or in a public place, I will get up and leave. I will not be humiliated by having to watch him stare at another woman. I also strive to do this without making a scene or being verbally abusive.* As a spouse, you don't have to be humiliated in this way. This is a good boundary to have. Be firm and let him know how it makes you feel. This can be done without verbal abuse.

3. *I will listen with my eyes. His words have been lies for so long that I will only believe them if they are consistent with his actions.* One action can be consistent attendance at group recovery meetings - going even when he feels like not going, going even when he has had a slip, going even when he might be upset with his wife, going if he hasn't done his homework.

4. *If he is continually late coming home, I won't prepare meals for him.* The objective isn't to set yourself up as his mother. It's a way of saying that you won't enable irresponsible behavior.

5. *I can have personal goals and dreams. Part of my program will be to work towards those goals and continue to improve myself. I don't have to feel guilty about taking care of myself.* Make priorities for yourself. Taking care of yourself isn't selfish. Much of your energy may have been invested in taking care of everyone else in your life while neglecting

yourself. Reba McEntire sang a song and made a movie called, "Is There Life Out There?" It was about a lady who had put all of her energy into her family and wanted to go back to school. She struggled with guilt, and the family had to make adjustments. But it was ultimately a great thing for the entire family. Taking time to explore your own dreams doesn't mean that you neglect your family. There can be room for both.

6. *I can have boundaries around my time. It's ok for me to do things for myself. Part of my program has been distinguishing selfishness from self-care.* The more you practice, the easier this will get. Your needs may have been neglected as you were enmeshed with others. Boundaries like this will help you develop a more balanced lifestyle.

7. *I won't rescue my wife from the consequences of her behavior. I've bailed her out because of my own shame. I need to let her feel the impact of her choices.* The most difficult addict to work with is one that has never experienced consequences. This man had rescued his wife so many times that he enabled her addiction to grow. He wouldn't let her experience consequences, believing that this would eventually make her stop. Once she experienced the pain she was causing, her recovery was ready to begin.

8. *I will stop pretending that nothing is wrong when something is clearly not right. I will communicate with emotional honesty and will tell him the truth about my feelings.* Spouses of addicts have second-guessed themselves and can get to where they question their own reality. Emotional honesty is part of developing an intimate relationship.

9. *I will use boundaries as a way to protect myself. I will check them out with my support network to make sure I am not being punitive.* Boundaries are set in place to protect you as a spouse; not to inflict punishment or revenge.

10. *I will not have sex until we are both tested for sexually transmitted diseases and have received the results.* If there is a chance that you (your spouse) could have an STD, don't

endanger yourself until you know that sex with your partner is safe.

Boundary Crashing

1. *I made myself miserable going through his phone records, credit card bills, searching his car, and checking his computer. I decided to surrender these things and focus on my own journey.* Search and seizure makes you miserable as a spouse. Trust can't be developed on the basis of spy reports. There will always be one more thing to search.

2. *I won't spend hours watching his girlfriend's house. I wasted a lot of time and felt miserable. He says he broke all contact. Even though I have doubts at times, I'll talk about them with people in my group or my sponsor.* Surrendering the illusion of control is one of the most difficult parts of the journey. The fear that you feel is real. He has given you reason to doubt. This will get easier as you go, but at first it will be extremely hard to let go.

3. *As tempting as it may be, I will not kick down the door of his lover's house or contact her in any way. After the first time I called her, I got angrier and more frustrated than ever before. I realized after I kicked my way into her house that I could've been arrested.* None of these things helped. The addiction wasn't about her, it was about him. And she could've ended up in legal trouble. Revenge on an affair partner may feel good temporarily, but it won't heal your wounds. More often than not, it makes them worse.

4. *I will surrender my ability to control him. I can't know where he is all of the time. I've gone through his wallet, pants pocket, dresser drawers, briefcase, daytimer and anything else I could find to help me feel that he was where he was supposed to be.* As hard as this is, letting go of control is the way to freedom. No matter how hard you try, you can't prevent him from acting out.

5. *As hard as it is, I am committed to not berate him or verbally abuse him in front of family, friends, coworkers, and people at*

church. My goal is to tell my story – not his. Focusing on the addict takes valuable energy – energy that could be used for your own recovery. Finding healthy ways to express yourself, your pain, and your emotions is a critical part of your healing. Verbal abuse keeps you focused on the addict.

6. *I will stop calling his sponsor, his group members, and leaders trying to pump them for information. Even if they answered my questions, I would still not be satisfied.* If they answered your questions they would be breaching a sacred trust of confidentiality. There will never be enough answers to satisfy the fear and vulnerability in your heart.

Treasures Of The Soul

Boundaries are about you protecting your heart. They are to be honored. One of my colleagues refers to them as "treasures of the soul." Your heart is precious and deserves the best of care. The heart pumps lifeblood throughout the body. Marriage is a place of vulnerability. To be open and vulnerable, safety must be created. Boundaries will help you create the safety you need so that you can open your heart wisely, not blindly, in your journey. Keep your heart healthy by protecting it with good, flexible boundaries. Let the good stuff in while keeping the bad stuff out.[47] Hearts that are shielded from people with rock walls won't experience the intimacy that they need. Hearts that are left unprotected will be trampled. Open your heart slowly and wisely, and experience the love, growth, and intimacy that God designed in marriage.

Chapter Nine

Healing In Community

Ann was terrified. She recently learned of her husband's sexual acting out with pornography and prostitutes. She longed to share her pain, yet feared that her story was unique and that nobody could possibly understand her fear and shame. "Why should I go to a group? He's the one with the problem. I don't need any more public humiliation. If he can fix his problem things will be ok. I tried listening to other people's stories but it was too depressing. It makes me angry all over again."

Ann's story is what we often hear as spouses begin to seek help and support. Recently, a spouse came to me telling of her recent experience in a local support group for spouses. Most everyone in the group began their own treatment almost one year from the time their husbands started recovery. Spouses are enduring extraordinary levels of pain in isolation, especially during the first year of the journey. The level of tolerance to emotional pain can be frightening.

Recovery doesn't take place in isolation. Nobody recovers by themselves. Healing will always take place in a community. The greatest therapist in the world cannot take you through this journey successfully without the support of others.

Nobody recovers by themselves.
Healing will always take place in a community.

Yes, it's true. You have been treated unjustly. You are experiencing the consequences of someone's sin and you are not to be blamed for his/her choices. This doesn't mean that you don't need help. Suppose you are injured in an automobile accident. The accident wasn't your fault and you weren't driving the car. Would that stop you from seeking treatment? Of course not. You would go to the hospital and have your wounds treated. Emotional wounds work the same way. As a spouse, friend, or family member of an addict, you have felt the consequences of their behavior. Focusing on the addict's behavior can become a way to avoid dealing with your own pain. But your pain is real. The devastation is overwhelming. Some spouses watch their husband/wife go to group each week, make phone calls, and interact with their support network. He/she comes home challenged, encouraged, and grateful that they have help with the struggles of the journey. As a spouse, you deserve the same. You need the support of others who are in the same boat. Navigating the rapids and obstacles of a river is draining physically and emotionally. By yourself, the boat may capsize and leave you floundering. When you share the burden of steering the boat with others, the rapids aren't as difficult to handle. The danger level goes down.

Have you ever noticed how geese fly? They will fly in the shape of a "V" in the sky. By flying in formation they work together to reduce the wind drag. When one bird tires, another rotates to the front where the wind drag is the greatest. The birds in the rear honk to encourage the others in the front to keep flying. If a bird falls out of the group, others will fall out with him to ensure his protection. By working together they get where they are going.

For spouses who have husband's who are not in recovery, you will need the support of a group to take your own journey. It's painful to hear stories of other spouses who have husband's who are working their program, knowing that your husband has yet to acknowledge that he has a problem. The feeling of loneliness and despair is great. The grieving is great as you face the reality that your husband may choose not to get well. It will be tempting to isolate. As difficult as it is, stay in community. It will help you heal as you accept your powerlessness over the addict.

Focusing on the addict's behavior can become a way to avoid dealing with your own pain

"Two are better than one, because they have a good return for their work. If one falls down, his friend can help him up. But pity the man who falls and has no one to help him up!" (Ecclesiastes 4:9-10). Who is in your support network? Do you keep a list of phone numbers and email addresses so that you can contact a safe friend whenever necessary? How do you stay out of isolation? The more alone you are, the more likely you will seek false solutions. No one takes this journey without stumbling. As the writer says, when you are in fellowship, a friend can pick you up when you fall.

Finding A Safe Community

Building new relationships may feel like a ball and chain as you start your journey of healing. It's tough to seek out others when you feel like becoming a hermit. Plus, finding a safe community presents challenges. Well-meaning people may make hurtful statements and do irrational things. It may feel like nobody understands.

Developing a support network is not optional if you are to recover. It's rare for a therapist to use words like "always" and "never." We aren't fond of universal generalizations. This is one time where it's appropriate. Nobody recovers in isolation. Every spouse must have a group or they won't survive. These friendships will be the source of healing. Let's consider some of the benefits of a support network, and how to manage some of the challenges of finding a group.

Coping With Shame And Isolation

As was said earlier, shame is a way of remaining enslaved to self-destructive messages and situations. As you discover that you aren't the only person struggling with life with a sex addict, you will find that the shame lessens. The deeper the shame the more isolated you will be. With isolation comes danger.

When the journey is experienced alone, the sense of victimization is reinforced. Acceptance of this victim identity will contribute to tolerating high levels of emotional pain. When your identity is that of a victim, it will keep you in unhealthy roles in relationships. Minimizing extraordinary pain can become common.

One spouse came to me talking of her many suicide attempts beginning at age 13. She spoke of her attempts to take her own life in a matter-of-fact tone of voice. She minimized high levels of emotional pain as a way to cope. When Cynthia got into the group, she shared her attempts to take her own life. The reactions of the others were enough to make her realize that she was denying the depth of her own pain. Marrying a sex addict was just one more painful thing to experience in life. She felt she deserved what she was getting, as men had always abused her. Remaining a victim was comfortable. It kept Cynthia from having to take action on her own issues. The group helped her to see how she had developed an identity as a victim. With their support, she began to set boundaries with her husband and experienced a sense of empowerment for the first time in her life. Had she continued in the victim role, this change would have never occurred.

Remaining in isolation keeps spouses from seeing the extent of the problem and the seriousness of what they are facing. When you are alone in the middle of a problem, your perspective will be limited. When you operate with tunnel vision, it is easy to get blindsided by more trauma. When you are flying with a team, the odds of noticing and protecting yourself from incoming danger will be much greater. Solutions to problems become clear when you can broaden your perspective. Limiting your vision often results in pain that could have been avoided. When I meet a spouse who feels "stuck", I often find that he/she is remaining in isolation.

Rationalization of the addict's behavior may intensify during times of isolation. The need for support and accountability during these times can't be emphasized enough. It's easy to blame yourself for the choices of the addict; especially if you've been used to the role of victim. Jane shares her experience of rationalizing during isolation in the early months of her journey.

"After I learned about my husband's affairs and his escapades with prostitutes, I refused to speak to anyone for the next nine months. I got depressed and drank a lot. It must have been my fault. I was a nag. I should've done a better job around the house. Maybe if I had just gone to the strip club with him like he begged me to, he wouldn't have cheated on me. I felt I didn't have a right to be mad, angry, or even hurt. It was my fault."

Jane's words show how the mind can play tricks on us when we have time to obsess. She blamed herself for things she had no control over. Her isolation fueled her cycle of irrational thinking. When Jane began working on her own recovery, she experienced struggles with slipping back into self blame. In group, she was able to have other spouses hold her accountable, and support her in the process of challenging these irrational thoughts. Eventually, she got to a place where she realized that she had no control over the decisions of others. Jane began to experience her own personal empowerment and began to abandon the role of victim.

Emotional Dishonesty

Emotional dishonesty has become a lifestyle for spouses of addicts. It's easy to say that things are ok when in reality they aren't. It may be that you have told the addict in your life that you felt your marriage was going well in an effort to avoid conflict. Or it may be that you led someone to believe that their behavior was acceptable, when in reality you were uncomfortable with the way you were treated. A group can provide a community of accountability that can help you break these patterns. As you interact with other spouses, they will be able to help you see things you would never see otherwise.

Developing emotional honesty is a challenge. A pattern many spouses struggle to break is unhealthy emotional "stuffing." From years of working with spouses, I've seen that most have never developed an emotional vocabulary. Emotions may be denied or minimized. A group can provide a safe place to develop an emotional vocabulary and develop healthy ways to cope with feelings.

Coping Skills

Jane's story reveals two of her pre-recovery coping skills. Isolation was how she coped with trauma since she was a small child. In her teenage years, she discovered that excessive drinking could numb the pain that she experienced from being sexually abused by an uncle. A therapy group can help you identify unhealthy coping skills and provide a safe place to practice new ones.

Take a moment and write down all of the ways you cope with stress, pressure, and trauma in your life. Recently we began asking spouses to list every form of coping they could remember using throughout life. Some of the things listed were:

1. Binge eating
2. Drinking
3. Shopping
4. Screaming
5. Rage
6. Hiding
7. Masturbation
8. Affairs
9. Marijuana
10. Isolation
11. Talking excessively
12. Avoiding the issue
13. Trying to "sell" my point of view so others would join me
14. Excessive smoking
15. Blaming
16. Sexual fa;ntasy

As the group develops, new coping skills can be developed and practiced in a safe setting. The group will provide a place for safe interaction with others. It's a chance to learn to reparent the child inside of you, who may have been abandoned or abused. Groups bring a power to the healing process that will exceed your expectations.

In addition to confronting trauma, you will need to celebrate success. The parties I've seen in our spouses groups are wonderful celebrations of progress. The victories are milestones that can keep you motivated during the difficult parts of the journey.

Experiencing genuine affirmation may be a first for you. Learning to receive compliments may be a challenge. How do you receive compliments? Do you find yourself minimizing them? Or perhaps you believe you don't deserve them and talk yourself out of receiving. We get used to one way intimacy. Do you find yourself doing most of the giving in your relationships with the addict? Others? These are patterns that contribute to perpetuating the cycle of craziness.

Consider the story of Jesus and Peter in John 13. Jesus is washing the feet of his disciples. When he comes to Peter and tries to wash his feet, Peter turns him away and tells Jesus that he can't wash his feet. Jesus tells Peter that unless he allows him to wash his feet, he can have no part of him. Peter then has a change of attitude. One of the lessons from this story is that we are not only to be servants, but we must learn to receive. The latter can be more difficult, especially for someone like me who has struggled with codependency. It's easier to give than to receive at times. The group will give you a safe place to practice.

Groups bring a power to the healing process that will exceed your expectations.

I victimized myself many times by wanting to be in the giving role constantly, and not being able to receive. Irrational giving, spending, and other forms of one-way intimacy led ultimately to feelings of resentment and frustration. It was the support and accountability found in a group that helped me overcome these patterns. It was also a safe place to learn to receive.

It's been almost 15 years since my first group experience. I was preparing to take a course in group counseling in graduate school, and I found myself experiencing a high level of anxiety about this class. I decided that the best way to confront this anxiety would be to join a group. It ended up being one of the most therapeutic experiences I've ever had. The class became one of my favorites. The group bonded so well that we all hated for the class to end. I was able to see patterns in my own life that I wouldn't have noticed without the group. And some of the patterns I spoke of in chapter two were things I learned while in there. It was in group that I realized I enjoyed the victim role too much. It kept me from taking responsibility for my choices. The group began to show me that deep levels of friendship and intimacy were possible without subjecting myself to the abuse of people who only wanted to use me. It was in group that I broadened my circle of friends. I would describe the denomination I grew up in as being somewhat isolated and incestuous. Anyone outside of my denomination was to be feared. I isolated myself from many people who could have been good friends, simply because they were from a different denomination. Being in community showed me that I could find safe people outside of my religious heritage. Today, most of my closest friends are from religious backgrounds other than mine.

It has been rare that I have ever seen a spouse regret joining a therapy group. The only complaint I ever get on our groups is that the spouses hate to see them end. The spouses build friendships that begin to meet their needs. I've watched them develop friendships that have a level of depth that people deeply desire. Issues of trust, intimacy, and boundaries can heal in group.

Keeping Each Other Warm

Contrary to popular opinion, men and women have more in common than not. Sexual addiction is not just about sex, but about a longing for intimacy and connection. And sexual acting out creates the illusion of closeness with another person. Desperate behaviors that spouses get into may be serving the same function. People typically don't like to be alone. We long for security and connection in relationships. Much of the pain of infidelity is when a spouse realizes that she wasn't that special someone who was chosen. Something that she should have had all to herself has been given away. The sense of betrayal and shock is overwhelming. No matter how deep the hurt, we still long for the closeness and intimacy that marriage represents. As we process the hurt, there is a strong need to develop healthy connections with others going through similar experiences. The needs of intimacy can be met through the group process.

In the early 1990's the Berlin Wall fell and the doors of opportunity opened for missionaries to work in the former Soviet Union. I met a lady who had been raised in Siberia. Her family had been murdered during the regime of Joseph Stalin. She was raised in an orphanage that was run by some rough characters. When children at the orphanage misbehaved, they were often forced to spend the night outside in the snow without any clothing. Many of the children died. Those who survived did so by huddling together around one child. They took turns being the one in the middle and kept each other warm. Those who left the group died quickly, while many of those who stayed close survived.

As you take the difficult journey of recovery, there will be times when you feel like those children. Cold, alone, fearful, hurt, treated unjustly, and abused. During these times, your group can surround you and keep you warm, motivated, and on the road to healing. As you experience your own personal growth, something else is going to happen. You will notice that people with similar struggles will suddenly seem to come out of the woodwork and find you.

As you take the difficult journey of recovery, There will be times when you feel like those Children. Cold, alone, fearful, hurt, treated Unjustly, and abused.

Brenda came to me ten years ago after being betrayed by her husband of almost 30 years. She shared many of her tears as we began to work through a long process of grief and healing. After Brenda went through a year of therapy, she called to tell me that women who had similar experiences were suddenly calling her for help. Many wounded people came through Brenda's house on the way to my office. She became an instrument of healing for many, and continues to this day. She is keeping people warm just as others did for her. Brenda discovered through this process that intimacy is a two way street. It involves both giving and receiving, something she didn't do in her first marriage.

Types Of Groups

There are different types of groups you can join. Because there are groups for different needs, it's important to understand the role that each can play in your journey. This section will provide some practical information on what you can expect from different kinds of groups. I'll also try to share how Faithful and True – Atlanta conducts and uses their groups.

Therapy Groups

Therapy groups will be led by a trained counselor who specializes in treating families of sexual addicts. These groups may be time-limited (a start and stop date). Some are ongoing. Therapy groups are not free. You will typically pay anything from $30 – $70 per session. The number of people participating is usually limited to 6-8. There will often be reading assignments and a variety of homework activities. You will probably do work around issues such as your family of origin, trauma, boundaries, and practical tools of recovery. Expect these groups to be intense and rewarding. The structure of the Faithful and True – Atlanta spouses groups involves a 16 week therapy group. It is limited to 8 spouses and involves a variety of therapeutic activities. It is designed to provide all of the basic tools a spouse needs to begin a journey of recovery.

Process Therapy Groups

These groups are also led by trained counselors, but they may focus on the specific needs of a particular group. Some of our groups have been impacted more by spiritual abuse, and wish to do additional work around this issue. Others may continue in a therapy group for sexual abuse survivors. Groups may meet weekly, bi-weekly, or monthly depending on the needs of the group. Faithful and True – Atlanta provides long-term therapy groups for survivors of sexual abuse, boundaries, codependency, and spiritual abuse. There are also weekly meetings designed to keep people connected. Members are expected to meet and interact throughout the month outside of group meetings, and are held accountable for building relationships and completing assignments.

L.I.F.E. Groups

L.I.F.E. Ministries International provides resources for people to start support groups. The L.I.F.E. guide for spouses, by Melissa Haas, is an excellent resource for starting a support group. These groups may be started by two spouses working the L.I.F.E. guide together. There is a facilitator's guide available to assist in beginning these groups.

Based on the work of Mark Laaser, there are seven L.I.F.E. principles designed to help people in recovery. For more information, visit L.I.F.E. Ministries on the web at www.freedomeveryday.org.

12-step groups

Based on the work of Bill W. and Alcoholics Anonymous, 12-step groups have saved the lives of millions of people. There are 12-step groups for sexaholics and their families. S-Anon is a 12-step fellowship for spouses and family members of sexual addicts. These are groups that are peer-lead and are very structured. Typically, someone will read a statement of purpose and group rules. There is a language that you will learn that is unique to 12-step meetings. Reading the S-Anon blue book will provide you with some of these terms. For example, meetings don't allow "cross-talk." Members will share without receiving feedback during the meeting. A collection basket for donations may be passed around at group meetings to cover the cost of rent and literature. Finding a sponsor will be critical in working the 12 steps.

Support Groups

Support groups may be generic or specific. They will typically be peer led, and are usually open for free or a small cost. Ask specific questions of the contact person to find out if spouses of sex addicts are appropriate for the group, how the group operates, etc... Support groups exist for a variety of issues and may take place in church or community settings.

Closing Thoughts On Groups . . .

Don't rely on one type of treatment. You will need individual counseling, group treatment, and ongoing support. The issues that surface in addicted families are complex and will require individual, group, and marital therapy. The people who seem to have the most success at Faithful and True - Atlanta have been through individual & marriage counseling. They will also typically do one of our experiential couple's retreats (see www.faithfulandtruemarriages.org for more information on these weekends). A spouses group is often where the journey begins. But those who spend 2-5 years in a combination of groups, individual, and couples counseling seem to have the best long-term success.

In closing, spouses groups are the most rewarding groups I have ever experienced. I love all of our groups at Faithful and True – Atlanta. Nothing is more rewarding to me than to experience this journey with our spouses and to see the transformation that takes place in their lives and marriages. As a therapist, I'm convinced that a solid therapy group will take six months off of individual therapy. So much can be accomplished in safe community. Even if you have had years of experience in individual therapy, consider joining a group. It will help you take your journey of recovery to a depth never before experienced.

Chapter Ten

Your Grief Will Turn To Joy:
The Forecast

...you will grieve, but your grief will be turned into joy.
                                                          John 16:20

One of the ladies in our spouses group who knew I was writing this book said that a great need for her and her husband was to hear what it's like on the other side. What does a spouse look like who has experienced some of the healing journey? I felt the best way to honor her request was to ask some of my clients to offer their personal testimonies. We have changed the names to protect the anonymity of the people who have graciously and generously offered to share their journey with you.

Spouses don't always end up in the same place. I have found that when both an addict and spouse make the decision to do individual and couples recovery that the marriages not only survive, they thrive. The reality is that not all marriages will survive. For that reason, we have included a variety of stories. In this chapter, you will hear from spouses that have experienced recovery and healing in their marriages, those whose marriages didn't make it, male spouses of female sex addicts, and those who are new to the journey. Realize in reading these stories that each person's journey is unique. These are a few examples of people known personally to the authors who have done much hard work in their individual journeys. Notice as you read them that you will see all of the elements of recovery and healing described in this book: Counseling, marital therapy, family work, therapy groups, support groups, ongoing contact with others in recovery, and many other tools and resources. Make notes on things that you need to explore in your own journey.

Marianne – A Voice That Will No Longer Be Silent

Everytime I heard the song "Amazed" by Lonestar, I wanted to cry. I didn't cry easily, so the emotion surprised me. The song writer seemed to have plucked the words of the lyrics out of my own love story. ...*Every little thing that you do, I'm so in love with you...* I turned the words over in my heart just to feel their weight. *I want to spend the rest of my life, with you by my side* . . . Was I being overly sentimental or nostalgic? After all, in less than 6 months my husband and I would be celebrating our 25th wedding anniversary. Why did I want to cry? My heart seemed to have a knowledge that my mind couldn't reach. I tried to grasp the reason. It must be the "empty nest" syndrome sneaking up on me. After all, my son just graduated from college and got married, and my oldest daughter was planning to leave for a 2 year ministry program in a few days. It could be that I was dreading the teenage years my youngest daughter was beginning to journey into. Perhaps it was a pre-menopausal mood swing. Maybe I just missed my husband. His job did seem to have imprisoned him again and totally consumed his time over the last few months. I couldn't even catch him long enough to talk to him about it. He must have been really busy at work, because he didn't even return my calls. The song lyrics came to my mind again . . . *Forever and ever … Baby I'm amazed by you.* The emotions were there and I knew I had to express them, so I wrote him a letter.

The letter was 'the state of our union" address. In it I expressed the love we used to know, the best friends we used to be, and how time, work, and family responsibilities seem to have eroded the landscape of our marriage. I concluded the letter with, "I am in the market for a best friend. My first choice is you. Do you want the job?" I was sure this would get a heartfelt "O honey, I am so sorry I've been so busy." Then we would make plans to reconnect and spend more time together. It always seemed to take such an effort to circle the wagons around him and unplug him from work. His job had always been the family rival. Now I waited for the right time to present the letter.

The next day was the Saturday of Labor Day weekend, 2001. My husband was in and out most of the weekend. His job rarely allowed him to have weekends off. The first day he was off was Monday for the holiday. Our children were still asleep, when I showed him my letter. Time seemed to stand still as he read the words. I desperately searched his face for tenderness and warmth. His face was blank, the rim of his eyes were red. I couldn't read the expression. Then he spoke. He said that he was thinking of leaving me around January. I almost started to laugh because I thought he was joking; only he stayed so somber. I couldn't comprehend or make any sense out of what he was saying. I managed to ask, "Is there someone else?" He said no, he just thought he would like to live on his own for awhile. I blinked repeatedly as if clearing my eyes would help me understand his words. There was no way for me to wrap my mind around his desire to leave. A strange numbness crawled up my body. I remember feeling like I had been transported into another woman's life and hit by a train at the same time. Was this the same man that said he could live in a tent as long as we were together? The same man who would lie in bed and gently stroke my face, calling me his brown-eyed girl? This was the man to whom I had given my whole heart and now he was breaking it.

The next 5 days were a complete blur as I found out more of the sordid story. There was indeed another woman, and he was having an affair with her. He was seeing her during the work day, lunches, dinners, weekends, all shielded with lies that I swallowed because I thought he was working hard and long for the good of his family. I was angry with him, and myself. I was deeply, deeply hurt. Usually I found prayer to be a comfort in times of trouble, only I couldn't find the words. The only thing I could do was lift my eyes and say "God, I am so glad you are near to the brokenhearted, because my heart is broken."

The sobs and grieving came without warning and from a very deep place within. The crying had such a mournful sound and I couldn't stop it or control it. I felt like I was having open heart surgery without anesthesia. It was the dream of true love and happily ever after … dying. I have never known such pain, and could not hide my emotion from my children. It must have been hard for them to see such agony in their mom.

Two more weeks passed and I began to see a tug of war within my husband's heart. There seemed to have been some lucid moments where he felt the weight of what giving up his family would mean. He agreed to go with me and see our pastor. We sat in the living room of our pastor's home. I knew that this would be the turning point or the breaking point. Our pastor proceeded to ask questions and confront and advise. Then we stood and pastor prayed for us. My husband looked me in the eye at the end of the prayer and for the first time in a long time I saw the man I used to know staring back at me. He said he was sorry and he would put an end to the affair. As we left our pastor's home he told us two things. First that I should be present in the room when my husband breaks off the affair and there shouldn't be any further contact with the other woman. Second he told us he was taking us out of our ministry positions in the church until we finished working out our marriage problems. I was extremely grateful for my husband's new frame of mind but something else died in me that I was yanked out of the ministry that I loved. I began to feel that I had a huge "scarlet letter" tattooed to my chest where the church was concerned. The two things that identified my life at this time were my marriage and family, and my ministry and church relationships. As the days went on I began to ride the wildest roller coaster ride of my life. My husband ended the affair and the other woman became vindictive, causing him to lose his job. I discovered that my husband had been addicted to Internet pornography for several years. When I went to church, people bombarded me with questions about why my husband and I were no longer in ministry. I didn't want to lie, yet I couldn't tell them the truth either. Our pastor basically turned us loose with no direction as to how, or where we could work on our marriage problems. I felt very alone, and it hurt . . . . bad. Up and down I went over the hills and valleys of the emotion, the addiction, the alienation, the betrayal, the sin. I no longer knew who I was. Everything in my life that seemed to define me no longer existed. My perfect dream had ended. My knight had fallen off his horse. There were no more sunsets to ride off into. As I disentangled myself from the enmeshed dream of true love and happily ever after, I looked toward the horizon. Where there used to be a sunset, I now see a dawn. I see the light of a new day and a new dream. I used to think that losing my marriage would be a tragedy. Now I know that the greatest tragedy in my life would be NOT TO FIND MYSELF!

It took over four years for me to find a group. I felt abandoned by the church, our pastor and was very alone. Now that I've begun my journey with a group of supportive and wonderful ladies, I wouldn't trade it for anything. God continued to reveal himself to me in ways that have been healing the hurts of the past. I'm grateful that I can share my story and that I have a voice.

Jill – Coping With Life As A Spouse, Even After Divorce

I turned thirty on my last birthday. I never was bothered by passing time, but this birthday hit hard. My life does not look like I thought it ever would. Never in a million years would I have ever imagined this. It had started off so serenely.

By the age of nineteen I was married. This man was everything I could have hoped for. He really had his head on straight and knew what he wanted to do in life. What a difference from all the immature college guys I saw every day. We struggled in the first few years of marriage with issues of communication and intimacy, but who doesn't? I decided my expectations were too high. I wanted to be a supportive wife, not a discouragement to him.

Four years into our marriage we had our first son, and a surprisingly short 7 months later, we discovered that we were pregnant again! The pregnancies and babies did not help our difficulties with intimacy. I had obviously set expectations of my husband's involvement way too high (again). Any difficulties that we had with deep, close connections were magnified during that time. He worked hard all day and wanted some time alone with me. Although I was frustrated with his lack of <u>awe</u> for our amazing little boys, he did have a point didn't he? I realized I needed to do better. Maybe if I could get everything in my day finished before he came home I would be more available to him and he wouldn't be so frustrated. Maybe I could keep him from emotionally shutting down. I was getting very tired, but I was determined to meet my husband's needs.

It was right around that time when I first found him cheating on the Internet. I felt the presence of evil in the room. It felt like a heavy weight that had suddenly fallen on my heart. It took hours of repeated questioning before he confessed to an addiction to Internet porn and "romantic" chat rooms. That was the beginning of the confessions. In fact, it turned out that my husband was actually very good at confessions. He begged for forgiveness, confessed to our pastor and went into counseling. It seemed to be a true repentance. And it appeared to be true repentance every single time he confessed to another period of unfaithfulness, for the next three years. His sorrow was deep and heart-felt, his promises were encouraging, and there was always a wonderful time of growing intimacy until he would begin to fade away again into his addiction.

I knew that as a Christian wife it was my duty to forgive, trust, to understand, and to pray for my husband. I did not know what to do with my feelings of fear and bitterness, but I believed those feelings were wrong and whatever problems I had in loving my husband were my problems. He needed prayer, he needed encouragement, he needed a supportive wife. My husband would reassure me of his faithfulness and his close relationship with God (he did read his Bible almost every day). He would even commit to pray for me and the state of my heart, so any hatred that bubbled up in my throat was obviously sin on my part. I tried to believe him. I tried to accept what he was telling me, but my heart had been broken. I was confused and I was miserable, but I was going to be a good wife no matter what.

Something happened that flipped a switch in my brain. I did not want the rest of my life to look like this. Did this come when I realized that all his assurances were lies? Was it when his addiction branched out past what he could do within our own home, and he finally met a woman in a hotel room? Was it when we went to counseling and began to learn about the destructive cycle in which my husband and I were involved? Or was it when we separated and the cloud of co-dependence started to clear? I'm still not sure. But I do know that somewhere along the line I came to understand my thinking was damaged. One morning I woke up and called my counselor to tell him I had realized something at about 4:30 a.m. I, too, was an addict. I was addicted to him. I believed that if I loved my husband enough, if I really understood him, if I met all his needs, if I prayed for him enough, he would be able to love me back. If it hadn't worked in the past, it was because I didn't do enough and I would have to try harder. Unfortunately, I could never do enough. I kept falling short, tiring out, repenting, and trying again. This thinking was a trap and it was driving me insane. It kept me from seeing the truth: My husband was unfaithful and we were both putting the responsibility on me.

I began to understand this. He did not. He did not understand it when we went through intensive addiction counseling and he wanted me to have compassion on him. He did not understand it when we separated-he wanted me to trust him again. He did not understand it when I told him I wanted a divorce-he couldn't believe that I would sink to such depths. To the very end of our relationship he kept saying that I was doing this to him. I knew that he had broken his vows to me, that he had left me and our children over and over again. He did it in his heart and in his mind. He had abandoned us. As I divorced him I was not choosing to end our marriage; he had already done that. I was just making the truth visible. I clearly remember him standing in front of me, telling me that what he had done was wrong, but would not result in permanent damage unless I chose to make it so. He told me that I was destroying our marriage and family by divorcing him, and that I would have to stand before God and answer for what I had done. I realize I was willing to do that.

It is obvious that my struggle with co-dependant behavior did not end with my marriage

I was scared the first year or so and I had to remind myself that being on my own was better than living in lies and insanity. I had seen and understood Truth and Life and, as it says in Philippians 3:16, I wanted to keep "living by the same standard to which we have attained." But I was often overwhelmed by fear and stress. I was a single mom now and had to raise two boys on my own. I worried about my children growing up in a broken home. I would have the overwhelming desire to compensate for that loss and to control my life. I wanted to do more, to do better, and to create a healthy, safe home and life for my children. I would find myself drifting toward "addictive" behaviors: I would have one too many glasses of wine at the end of the day, I would watch too much television, I would start eating too much or shopping too much, or even reading too much. I would do about anything to shut off the constant worrying and fixing and list-making in my brain. If I prayed enough, organized enough, explained enough, could I make things better for them? Could I fix their lives? Could I keep them safe?

It is obvious that my struggle with co-dependant behavior did not end with my marriage. I recognize it in my thinking and choices all the time. It is scary to learn all the things I do not have control of, but there is a deep peace in the practice of trusting God.

I am thirty years old now and I realize that I have a lot for which I am very thankful. Some days I wake up and have a feeling of lightness, of freedom. I see the whole day stretched out in front of me as a huge blessing. I see the wonderful job God graciously laid in my lap. I see the house He allowed us to buy. I see my boys growing, fighting, laughing, learning, and I am grateful that I am sane enough to enjoy it all. I am grateful that it is not up to me to keep the world spinning. I don't always remember that, but it comes to mind much more quickly now. There is peace and there is rest.

Melvin – The Story Of The Male Spouse Of A Female Sex Addict

I was devastated. I couldn't believe that she would do this to me. For me, my nightmare began about 9 months ago. I noticed Cindy was doing some things she never did before. She was coming home intoxicated. She was always working late and seemed to lose track of time. She started smoking, something which she had always hated in others. She became more withdrawn from the kids and we were all feeling neglected, though none of us knew how to express it. We didn't talk about emotions in our house very well, unless someone was really angry. I finally confronted her after seeing strange numbers on the cell phone bill. She denied it for what seemed like an eternity. Then she finally broke; and she admitted that she had been sleeping with many different men and women over the last 9 months. I couldn't believe it. I didn't know whether to collapse in shock or hit her. I just stood there staring at her, frozen in time. And she didn't seem real sorry. I began to beg her not to leave. I told her we could work things out and begged her not to embarrass or humiliate me. She made no promises. She tried to blame me at first, then everyone else in her life. She finally agreed to go to a counselor, provided I went and found one. That was the start of my journey.

The first counselor told me that I needed to be more sexual with my wife. She told me that even if I didn't feel like it, I needed to have sex with her whenever she wanted and do whatever she wanted me to do. This felt wrong, but who was I to question the wisdom of a woman with all of these letters after her name. Finally, my wife got tired of her and said she wasn't going back. I decided to seek help on my own. I attended a workshop for spouses in Atlanta. There were only two male spouses including myself, but the group quickly accepted us after getting over the initial shock of seeing men in the room.

I had been sexually abused by an older woman in school when I was 12 years old. I grew up in church and knew that this was wrong, but was terrified to tell anyone. The shame I experienced around the abuse was overwhelming, and I carried this secret until I was 35 years old. When my wife told me she was sleeping around, I felt so inadequate and ashamed. I blamed myself and didn't want to tell anyone. I discovered that the other man at the workshop felt the same way I did. Our group leader explained why the culture we live in makes it harder for a male to cope with being the spouse of a female sexual addict. I blamed myself for everything. If I'd only treated her better, been better in bed, done somersaults and handsprings, brought her flowers every day, etc. etc. etc... then maybe she wouldn't have done this. However, as I got into individual counseling after the workshop, I began to realize that the problem had nothing to do with sex. We had both been wounded as children and neither of us really knew how to be married.

We have just begun our couples counseling and it seems to be off to a good start. I no longer spy on my wife and I try not to check phone bills constantly. I let her share her journey with me and I share mine with her. I still mess up and want to interrogate her a little too much, and end up feeling miserable afterwards. But I am doing much better. I have now gone 6 months without checking her car for clues.

At the workshop, the other man who was there was about 7 years into his journey of recovery with his wife. He told me it took him about 2 years to get over all of the search, seizure, and spying activities. I'm grateful that he shared this with me. I now have a support group that helps me try to avoid destructive behaviors. I still go to my therapy and my wounds are beginning to heal. Though I don't know where the journey will lead, my wife and I have made a commitment to each other and surrounded ourselves with people who are taking this journey along with us. I am beginning to have more good days than bad ones. I don't get as depressed as I used to, and I now know it isn't my fault that my wife made the choices she did.

Janet – Facing Your Trauma As A Spouse

My journey began when I could not stand the pain of my husband's sex addiction any longer. In hindsight, I guess you could say that I had finally had all I could take. My husband was having an affair with a woman that used to work for him. My intuition had been telling me that fact for months. But my denial was stronger than my intuition. Finally, I confronted him. He admitted the affair and his love for her. Then he packed a bag and walked out the door.

I thought we had a good marriage. We did not fight very often. Our sex life was finally at a place where it was pretty consistent and good. We both had decent careers. We had a house. We laughed together. We had two small children. We went to church occasionally.

That was all before the affair started. Immediately after Stephen entered into a sexual relationship with Samantha, he changed dramatically. He started "meeting the guys" for golf. He started having after hour projects at work. He lost weight. He whitened his teeth. More importantly, he was gone - mentally and emotionally. Checked out. Disconnected.

His behavior triggered my deep fear of abandonment. My coaddiction kicked in to high gear. I started checking his cell phone. When he went to bed I would get up and look through his briefcase. I would check his email messages while he was in the shower. I knew something wasn't right. I finally found a way to get his company cell phone bill. I found out that he was calling her 30-50 times per day. I threatened divorce if he did not stop calling her. I lost weight. I bought sexy clothes. I had breast implants put in. I raged. I wanted him by my side every waking moment so I could monitor whether or not he was making calls. I called her. I called her husband. I called his Mom. I called my sister. My life had become completely unmanageable. I prayed on my face almost every day. I begged God to bring whatever it was into the light. And He did.

My husband called me the day after he walked out and he asked me not to file for divorce. He asked if he could talk to me. I agreed under the condition that he stop the affair and that we seek help from a Christian counselor. Within 30 minutes of meeting with a pastor at our church, we heard the term sex addiction. Now that we were at the truth, the real work would begin.

My work began when I came to realize that I had my own part in this. I had my own issues that had never been dealt with. They were deep and they hurt.

We began to learn about sex addiction through books and the Internet. I started attending L.I.F.E. group meetings for spouses. I will never forget the first time my therapist mentioned the term "co-addict." I thought that being a codependent, I could handle it. But my immediate reaction was "I am not a co-addict." Not me. That seemed to me at the time to symbolize more problems with me. Didn't I already have enough?

I began some deep family of origin work. I had a lot of wounds that had never been dealt with. Molestation by a close relative. My

Dad and step-Dad were alcoholics. My dad walked out on my Mom and did not make contact for 21 years. There was rape, emotional abuse by my Mom, Abandonment, and other deep stuff. This all brought up tremendous amounts of grief. Simultaneously I would go from shock to rage to depression daily, (sometimes minute-to-minute) in dealing with my husbands betrayal. I felt out of control. What happened to this supposed "happy life" I had? How could God let this happen to me? Hadn't I been through enough already? Could I trust Him now?

I started a daily devotional. I wrote in a journal. I met with my therapist weekly. I was making progress, but I still cried every single day. And I would wake up most mornings crying my eyes out. I had nightmares that he would leave and humiliate me again. It was a battle to focus on me and not on him and his addiction.

I kept going to a L.I.F.E. group for spouses of sex addicts. The first few meetings felt odd. There was a format that had to be followed. I couldn't just start commenting on someone else's feedback. There was no crosstalk. No one was going off about their husband. Instead, these women were talking about themselves. Sure they mentioned their addict. But in terms of how they were setting "boundaries" with him or how they were "taking care of themselves after letting themselves feel their feelings". They talked about calling each other for support. They talked about not worrying about tomorrow - we have all the resources we need to take care of today. Talk about foreign. I slowly began to realize that this is what healthy women looked like. They came from all ages, races, social status, and religious backgrounds. The common theme was helping each other stay out of their illness and focusing on their own well-being.

I was one of them. After a few meetings, I knew this was where I belonged. But I was afraid I would mess it up - that I would not say the "right" recovery thing. The last thing I needed was to be rejected by women I was supposed to feel safe with. Fortunately I never found any rejection. Instead, each woman accepted each other wherever they were. I found a L.I.F.E. group family.

While at home I still felt shame. I raged. I cried. I tried to figure out why he did what he did. If I could just figure that out, then maybe I could stop it next time. I felt sorry for myself. I wanted pity. I wanted someone/everyone to acknowledge that I was a victim here. I looked for my husband to validate me. I looked for my Mom - who had never nurtured me - to nurture me. Anything but turn from my pain.

But slowly, I started to get it. His disease was not about me. I did not cause it. I could not control it. All I could control was me.

God was revealing Himself to me, sometimes daily. I was broken. He started to rebuild me. He would lead me to places in His Word where I could find hope. He would lead me to places that would comfort me. I found my desire for Him start to increase. I was reading about how we had to go through trials to perfect our faith. I read that God sets prisoners free through trials. I began to realize that I had been a prisoner to my disease. My past held me captive.

I prayed for God to lead me to a sponsor. I prayed for a big sign or multiple signs because I still could not trust my intuition. He gave me the signs I needed. I found my sponsor. We started the work on the 12 Steps together.

Part of my disease was not completing things. I made up my mind that I was going to complete the 12 Steps in six days. I had to work on setting realistic expectations. My eyes opened to my powerlessness. I could see clearly how my life had become so unmanageable. I believed that Jesus could restore me to sanity. Most importantly, I learned firsthand that I could trust the Lord with my will and my life and that I knew that He would act in my highest good - that I did not have to be so vigilant about control. He was in control.

It was a battle, but slowly I started to let go. I realized that I could say "no" to people. I realized that I did not have to rescue people. I realized that I did not have to take certain kinds of treatment from anyone - including my mother. God was doing for me what I could not do for myself.

I joined a woman's organization that caused me to do some work around shame. Shame permeated my life. I felt shame about everything. I also learned that I had operated from my little girl self 90% of my life. I came to know my woman. I came to know that the Holy Spirit would guide my woman. I did not have to fear. She could have her own voice.

I have forgiven my husband and the woman he had the affair with. Not forgiving was only causing me more pain.

I am exactly where I am meant to be. Jesus set me free by causing me to walk through the fire. I still feel hurt. I still have a deep wound inside. There are days when I cannot believe what pain I have walked and am still walking through. But I can tell you that Jesus never left my side. I believe He allowed this to happen so that my life purpose might be fulfilled, and so that His will may be done.

Chapter Eleven

Redeeming The Pain – Hope For The Journey
(Debbie Whitcomb)

"They send this kind of stuff to everyone…I'll take care of it." Those words are the first I remember on a very long journey that continues to this day regarding my husband's addiction to pornography. A sales brochure had come in the mail showing books that had "dirty" pictures in them. I was appalled, but quickly reassured by my husband of less than a year that it was nothing to worry about. Being so kind and gallant, he would rescue me and handle it, he told me. I remember thinking how wonderful he was at taking care of me and protecting me. I had no knowledge of the addiction that had impacted him for almost 15 years. I didn't have a clue that the consequences of his addiction would be so devastating.

We have just celebrated our 34th wedding anniversary. I would love to be able to tell you that all has turned out well for us. Although our relationship is in the process of being restored and redeemed with God's grace and goodness, there continue to be valleys that we must walk through. My prayer is that my story will provide you hope and encouragement. I pray that you will come to know the Lord in a sweeter and deeper way than you have known possible. I would ask Him to show Himself new to you every morning. May He show you the wisdom and scope of His plan. I would ask Him to give you mighty inner strength through His Holy Spirit that comes from His glorious, unlimited resources. May Christ be more and more at home in your heart as you trust in Him. May your roots go down deep into the soil of God's marvelous love. May you have the power to understand, as all God's people should, how wide, how long, how high, and how deep His love really is. May you experience the love of Christ, though it is so great you will never fully understand it. Then, you will be filled with the fullness of life and power that comes from God. Remember He is able to accomplish infinitely more than you would ever dare ask or hope. (Eph. 3:14-21)

This was a promise shared with us from a dear friend. It has encouraged me so greatly. I trust it will cheer you on as well. As you read my story, I also pray that you will be keenly aware of how faithful, long-suffering and patient God has been.

This is huge for me. Up until recently, I had known love to be conditional. I had to be good enough for God to really take care of me and to treat me with His goodness. But through the events of my journey and the redemption of our marriage, He has shown me how full and complete His love can be. As painful as the journey has been, I am so thankful that He loves me enough to grow me more and more into His image. My Pastor once said, "He loved you enough to save you, but loves you too much to leave you in the state He found you." I have learned that He will go to any measure to have you know how precious you are to Him. He is indeed a jealous God and wants you to love Him and Him alone. He wants to meet your every need. He wants to be your El Shadai – your all sufficiency. I must be a stubborn child! But, thankfully, He is full of grace and simply loves me because He created me.

Living in a home with an individual who has a sexual addiction is confusing and perplexing on a good day! For years I felt things were not quite right in our marriage, but I didn't have the skills or tools to understand why and certainly didn't begin to understand how to "fix" the situation. There was a distance between my husband and me. There was a lack of emotional intimacy and connection. There were certainly good moments and pleasant events, but the more I looked to him to be my soul-mate and meet my emotional needs, the more separated we became. When he was happy and content, then I could be relaxed and peaceful. Once I had that formula figured out, I worked my life around making things go easily and peacefully. Then I was OK! My value, emotions, meaning of life were all centered on his response to me. If he was distant with me – I never knew why – I felt terribly alone and abandoned. My feelings and self perception revolved totally around his mood. In the course of the marriage, I lost who I was. However, in the past few years, I have re-discovered who I am as a child of God. I now see myself first in relationship to my heavenly Father, then in relationship to my husband. This is the correct order it needed to be all along!

I began seeking help for my marriage. I was still fairly clueless about sexual addiction, but realized I no longer choose to live in chaos and frustration. Prior to making that decision, pornography had greatly impacted our family. When our son was about 11 years old, I discovered him looking at pornography on the computer. I would like to tell you that I calmly discussed it with him – I didn't! I blew up at him, accused him of being deceitful and untrustworthy to have that on the computer. He told me it was a CD that had come from a friend. I threatened to call that boy's mother – everyone should know about this, I thought! Then, my son said it was really his daddy's pornography. I was shocked, angry, and scared. Then God restored some sense of reason to me, as well as compassion for my child. My son went on to say that he had found it and other things in a box. When I looked in the box, I was disgusted and sick that my husband had allowed our precious son to be exposed to this junk. Our son had been violated and abused by viewing the pornography. I know today that this event was sexually abusive to our son.

I was furious with my husband as I later told him the events of the day. He merely said he would take care of it and was sorry he left the box where our son could find it. He assured me he would get rid of it all. Again, I believed him and thought the problem had gone out with the trash; how naïve of me. I had no inclination of the depth of the addiction and the profound effects it would still have on all of us.

With the addition of the Internet into our home, pornographic images would pop up. My husband quickly dismissed it, telling me that they just get sent to you. I was so new with computers and the Internet, that it was easy for me to believe him once again.

Our sex life was minimal. It seemed to be mutual. He rarely initiated sex, except in the middle of the night. I ignored him for the most part, preferring to sleep. I felt rejected when he didn't respond to my initiations of sex. On the rare occasions we did have sex – 2-3 times a year – we both agreed we enjoyed it and should do it more often, but the pattern never changed.

After I had discovered the pornography, I felt he was turning to it because I hadn't responded to him sexually. In an attempt to be more appealing to him, I bought several new gowns, initiated sex more often, and responded to him every time he came to me. Yet the pornography continued. There came a time when we had sex every day, sometimes twice a day, for almost a month; while he was still involved with pornography. Surely, I wasn't enough for him. I believed I no longer had an allure for him. Little did I know that his longings were never for sex, but for an elusive emotional attachment that he found, or thought he had found, in pornography. I later learned that it was never about me in the first place. He was and would have been involved with pornography regardless of whom he had married. However, for years I truly believed that his attraction and addiction to pornography was my fault.

Very few friends knew about my husband's pornography attraction. I was too ashamed and embarrassed to discuss this. A few years later, when I was finally able to realize that this was more than a bad habit, as one counselor had told me, I began to seek help for myself. If my husband wanted to tag along, fine. But *I* was emotionally spent. I was tired of being in a marriage and still being alone. The help I was looking for was the "silver bullet" that would tell me how to fix my husband or find out how to live with him if he chose not to change. There was a period of time when I had convinced myself that it really wasn't all that bad, I would just have to adjust and make do. Who really had a fulfilled marriage, anyway? I just wanted the chaos, the "crazies" and the emptiness to go away. I was convinced that if I could find the solution, it would be resolved and the pain and heartache would go away.

That was my plan when I attended my first L.I.F.E. group meeting for spouses of sex addicts. They seemed like fairly normal women, maybe just a little too weak and whiny for me, but it looked like they might have some answers! I was willing to give it a try. It was comforting to know some of them were in worse marriages than mine! It was also reassuring to know that I wasn't the only one dealing with something like this. Prior to coming to this group, I had felt isolated and limited in my options. They spoke so honestly and matter-of-factly. How could they be smiling and laughing? Didn't they realize the seriousness of this problem? Maybe they really weren't emotionally sound after all.

I scrutinized them for weeks, rarely saying anything. Someone else new had asked how long it takes before the guys are "cured" of this addiction. They answered, "Never. They will deal with this addiction at some level for a long time. They will learn to make better choices. You will learn appropriate and safe ways to respond to their choices." I almost bolted for the door. Then why bother? I wanted out of the crazies, I wanted calm and peace and love, NOW. Was I correct in understanding sexual addicts never "graduate" from the program? This was not at all hopeful! Yet, I kept on returning, week after week – listening, taking it all in. I was confident that I was smart enough and disciplined enough to be one of the fortunate ones. I would be able to help my husband get over this, and we would carry on our lives unscathed. We would be one of the success stories. He would see the error of his ways, leave it all behind, adore me alone, our marriage would be a testimony to God's grace, and we would live happily ever after!

I remember being impatient with some of the ladies who, week after week, were complaining about the same problems and issues in their marriages. Why didn't they just get over it and move on? Did they have to continually re-hash their pain and feelings? I felt like singing with Barbara Streisand, "Feelings, nothing more than feelings!" Where was the victory in all of this? How was God being glorified in their lives if they couldn't move on? Come on, ladies!!!

During our feelings wheel check-in, I always shared my positive feelings...life was, after all, so much better than it had been. My husband was attending his L.I.F.E. group for male sex addicts. He was being open and relating to me. I was beginning to get to know him in a fresh new way. He was letting barriers down and our communication was really improving. It was indeed so much better, much calmer; and the "crazies" were all but gone. As long as he was on track, I was fine. How could I share anything but good feelings with the ladies' group? I eventually came to realize that I had forgiven too soon, was not even aware of what I had forgiven, and just wanted "normal" to return. I had not taken into account the cost of his addiction on our boys or on me. I was content and thankful to just have a calm and much more peaceful existence. But I was to discover God wanted more for me.

He wanted to allow me to experience His love, His adoration, His peace, His calm, His grace, His forgiveness, His joy, and His promises for an abundant life now. I was still finding my fulfillment in my husband, not totally in Him. As I said earlier, I have found Him to be a jealous God. He has not allowed me to have anyone but Him as my first priority. Not even my husband.

As I continued to attend the Spouse Group meetings, I heard them repeatedly say I couldn't control my husband's choices. (I had retired my private investigator badge – I no longer searched the computer, house, or car for clues to his pornography involvement.) What I could control were *my* reactions to the choices he made. I also learned that it was my responsibility to share my feelings with my husband. This meant positive as well as negative emotions. This is where one of the first challenges came. I had, for most of my life, stuffed my emotions and feelings inside. I had lost who I was. I continued to wear a mask, a façade, that all was well. I had become the poster child of how good God was. I believed He needed me to be Suzy Sunshine so the world would know how great He is! After all, if I wasn't happy, positive and excited about the wonderful changes He was bringing, how could I be a witness to the world? It was my duty! It was the least I could do for all He had given to me through His Son, Jesus! So, when my precious Christian sisters in the Group challenged me to be honest, transparent, and authentic with my feelings, that was extremely difficult. After all, the façade that all was well had been my coping mechanism for most of my life.

I had first learned to cover and mask my feelings as a very young child. I learned not to acknowledge my hurts or emotions. When I was five I was molested by a family member. I never told my parents about this. Instead, I just buried the shame and pain. For decades

I denied the impact the event had had on me. The truth was, I felt soiled and of less value after being sexually molested. However, I minimized the emotional and physical abuse of the act. I have now learned to acknowledge how that act had destroyed my innocence and impacted the way I perceived my worth. It led to behaviors as a child that cried for help, but were dismissed by my family. Through counseling, I learned that I had to forgive my parents for not protecting me as a young child. That was a difficult concept for me to understand. How could they have protected me if they didn't even know about it.

I also began to explore my anger issues! I had very proudly believed that I was not an angry individual. I never blew up – well, not in public; home was a different story. But I never flew off the handle. I was never violent. In fact, everyone often commented to me how I could see both sides of a situation and never loose control of my emotions. Yes, I was quite proud of myself for such tremendous self-control. Wow, then God allowed me to see several areas of truth. Pride was one! Then, the sin of being passively angry was revealed to me. Ouch! That truth hurt. It became apparent I had allowed that behavior to hurt many people, including my husband. It gave me an outlet to be in control, or so I thought. I had manipulated many folks.

When I first began recovery work, I truly believed that if my husband could "get over" this addiction, we would be fine! I did give God permission to make any adjustments in me that He felt would help. I knew I wasn't without any blame; but after all, the deep issues were my husband's. A few months into the program, however, I slowly began to see that I carried some issues as well. As I gained knowledge about the addiction, I was discovering that I also had a cycle of addiction. It felt abnormal if I wasn't stirred up about something. It didn't feel right to have things going along well for too long. I distinctly remember an occasion when I felt and appeared calm and was sensitive to how awkward that was. My "crazies" had become so normal to me that I actually grieved when they were not present. My reality was in a state of flux. I was not confident or qualified to respond at this new level.

Today, I continue to learn to recognize, admit, and explore my feelings. Sometimes the pendulum swings too far from the center, in my attempt to discover and explore how I really feel. But I have discovered such freedom and peace as I am becoming more skilled with transparency and authenticity in my emotions. With the support of my friends in the Spouse Group, I am acknowledging my feelings, even when they may not present the best face! It is alright to be sad, angry, hurt, anxious, and I have been encouraged to admit these feelings to others. I am not responsible for how others may react to my feelings. I am simply responsible to acknowledge my feelings and be honest about them.

As I listened to other women in my group discuss their struggles, I was keenly aware they were being real and searching for transparency in this arena. Their honesty about anger helped me. It scared me to know I had been out of control, even if it didn't look too bad to other people. Their continued honest and frank discussions showed me it was OK to have these feelings and emotions. I was uncovering a very freeing truth: I didn't have to be perfect! I also learned these ladies would continue to love me, warts and all.

Some time into our recovery program, my husband had several slips in his sobriety. We separated and continue to live apart. This has been a time for me to really encounter the Lord and seek His direction for my life and the future of our marriage. He continues to demonstrate His total sufficiency to me. He has surrounded me with friends and family for encouragement, financial support, and unconditional love; as well as challenged me to seek Him moment by moment.

Boundaries were instituted to protect me and to provide the time and environment for me to explore who I am in Christ. God has given me the opportunity to love and trust Him as never before. This separation phase was the catalyst to experience God's desire and ability to meet all my needs. I haven't been able to medicate by obsessing about husband. I have been required to address my issues, independent of my husband. We have both been on our separate recoveries.

During that time, we had been led to consider the future of our marriage. With all the pain and disappointment I had experienced, I was not certain if I could remain in the marriage. I questioned the love I had for my husband. I felt numb towards him. I didn't really like him and wasn't sure if I loved him. On several levels, it would have been simpler at the moment to have ended the marriage. I knew that I could not fabricate a love for my husband. If God intended for this marriage to be reunited, He will be the One to bring about a heart change in me.

My husband and I had limited visits during this time. These months have provided a cocoon for me to get to know who I am and to fully rely on God to meet all my needs. My husband might never be able to relate to me. I cannot depend on him, but I do have a powerful Father who is so able and willing to love me and to nurture me.

My husband and I do look to the future with a reconciled marriage. We have gone through a time of separation. This separation was a time to work on our issues with the goal of reconciling. God has indeed done a work in my heart to bring about a pure and honest love for my husband. Through no work of mine, God has restored in me a love for my husband. God has allowed me to be able to once again love him. This time, I have an unconditional love for my husband. The Lord has shown me this is the manner in which He has loved me – unconditionally, not seeking gain; while expecting the best in me. God has shown me that His love protects, hopes, and perseveres.

When my husband does return to the home, there will be further boundaries in place to protect me. While he is not in the home, I have been safe. When he returns, we will live as roommates, in separate rooms of the house. He will do his own laundry, prepare his own meals, and court me before I will be able to fully have a marriage relationship with him. He tells me this is his desire as well; that he looks forward to winning me back. I so want to believe him. But over the years I have learned that his words were not always believable. He will have to show me his intentions. In the movie, "My Fair Lady," there is a song where Eliza Doolittle sings to the man who is trying to court her. One of the lines goes, "Don't talk of stars, burning above. If you're in love, show me!" Spouses of men who struggle with sexual addiction are tired of words. They desire *actions that match words.* Another great expression from my Pastor is, "When the tongue in his mouth is going the same direction as the tongue in his shoe, then you have truth."

"One day at a time" is a saying we hear quite often. It is used in recovery circles. Honestly, I have cringed every time someone has said that to me. It has appeared so hollow and overly simplistic. Now however, it is the guidepost along the path of my journey. I certainly don't know how our future will come together. But, God is continuing to show me that His grace is sufficient for TODAY! It is not His plan that I know the outcome, just to rest in Him and wait for His timing.

I am often reminded of the Abraham and Isaac story. What a faith walk they had going up the mountain! I have recently been challenged to be honest with my "Isaacs." What are the "Isaacs" in my life that I need to present to God? Who are the people in my life that I might worship above the Lord? What are the possessions that I have made an idol in my life? God will not allow them to have first place. He calls me daily to lay everything down that would take my eye off of Him.

The Sunday school answer is that all things work together for good. But in my quest for honesty, transparency and authenticity I must share that this promise doesn't take away the pain of walking the road. So, my prayer is for God to be patient with me; to know my heart and to allow me to continue fleshing out my salvation with fear and trembling. I am not even able to have the ability to do that without His Holy Spirit. This is all about trust.

God continues to show us what His light is all about in this darkened world. There was once a dark cave, deep down in the ground, underneath the earth and hidden away from view. Because it was so deep in the earth, the light had never been there. The cave had never seen 'light.' The word 'light' meant nothing to the cave, who couldn't imagine what light might be. Then one day, the sun invited the cave to come up to the surface. When the cave came up to visit the sun, it was amazed and delighted; it was dazzled by the wonder of the experience. Feeling so grateful to the sun for inviting it to visit, the cave wanted to return the kindness. It invited the sun to come down to visit sometime, because the sun had never seen darkness. So the day arrived when the sun came down and was courteously shown into the cave. As the sun entered the cave, it looked around with great interest, wondering what 'darkness' would be like. Then it became puzzled, and asked the cave, "Where is the darkness?"

You see, light changes the very nature of darkness; and darkness cannot remain where there is light. I pray God's light of Christ will completely dispel the darkness in your life.

I thank God daily for the Truths I have grown to embrace through this journey. Have I enjoyed the trip? Not always! The pain has been almost unbearable on numerous occasions. However, had I not taken this journey, my relationship with the Lord would be no where approaching the intimacy that it has today. So, I do thank Him for walking me through the deep waters! They have never overtaken me. He has always made a path for me. He has always brought someone to walk along with me at my weakest moments – without fail, He has done this! He continues to be full of love and compassion. His mercies are new every day and His grace is sufficient for the day.

Through this journey, my husband has come to Christ for salvation! The men in his L.I.F.E. group introduced him to the One who could love him unconditionally and meet all his needs. For this one purpose alone, the journey has been invaluable and incredible. His relationship with Christ grows daily. Walking closely with Him is the means by which eternal changes will occur.

Relationships have flourished in other arenas. As I have become aware of the influences of my past, as I choose to be tenacious in continuing my recovery, I am uncovering the woman I really am. With this freedom, I can better connect with our children, family, work associates, friends at church, and my recovery community. Community is all important. God created us to be in relationship with Him and His children. It continues to be a moving and emotional understanding of all He has planned!

My pain has had a purpose. Today I am blessed to be a part of a fellowship of spouses on an incredible journey. We share our victories and our pain. I have relationships that would have never existed otherwise. I've learned that God has a purpose for me as I've struggled to make sense of things. I don't always understand why things happen, but I see God's hand in each struggle. Sharing my story has been redemptive in itself. I have been blessed to share it with many spouses in my L.I.F.E. group and with therapists, pastors, and church leaders who have attended sexual addiction treatment training events through Cornerstone Training.

God redeems pain. He is a God of redemption. I don't know what His purpose is for your pain, but he has....Discovering the good that can come is part of your own healing journey. May He bless you and keep you safe as you get to know yourself, your God, and the amazing ways He works in his children.

Debbie

Chapter Twelve

Pearls Of Wisdom:
Learning From The Voice Of
Experience

It's been over a year since the writing of S.A.R.A.H. began. Writing this book has been a journey that has had victories, defeats, traumas of invasion and abandonment, satanic attacks, frustration, joy, laughter, and tears. It comes to an end much as it began, with a vision and dream to provide something hopeful and useful to spouses of sexual addicts. Only, the dream and vision are greater than ever before. Experiencing the journey has led to greater resolve to stay with this mission. Tonight a new spouses group began at Faithful and True Atlanta. Once again, the pain, fear, insecurity, and agony of spouses beginning the journey were so clear. I grieve with those who experience the agony of discovering their partner's sexual addiction. I experience it with them as I look at the sheer agony on their faces and the tears in their eyes. As group leaders, we have cried with and for many of the spouses in our groups. Many times I have wished that there was a magic wand I could wave and make the pain go away. Magic wands only exist in fairy tales. Fairy tales make for great dreams. After the last "they lived happily ever after" there is a return to the real world. The movie ends and reality returns. There is no princess that lives forever and the good guy doesn't always win.

Throughout the work on S.A.R.A.H., I have been blessed to share in the journey of many spouses. Some of them have shared their stories in this book. I'm forever grateful to these ladies and gentlemen who were willing to be vulnerable and share their journey with you. They do so not knowing how it will be received. What made them take a risk like this? They care about every spouse who is reading this book. Their lives have been transformed and they are at a place where they want to share their journey. Each one shares in a mission to bring hope and healing to as many spouses as possible.

As I was graduating from college, I was also preparing to get married and enter full time ministry. When Vickie and I talked about these decisions, we decided that it would be good to talk with couples who had ministry experience. We wanted to find out what worked and what didn't. We were ridiculed by some for wanting to do this. We were able to talk to a couple of families who were in ministry, but we wish we had talked with more. It's rare that I will make a major decision today without listening to the voices of experience. I am a survivor. Some days I survive better than others. Whether the decision is related to career, family, parenting, money management, I want to hear from people who have been successful. Successful doesn't mean perfect. I want to know what worked and what pitfalls to avoid. Wisdom has been described as a great pearl. It needs to be highly valued.

The spouses who have shared their journey have given us great pearls of wisdom. Within their stories are the tools needed for a powerful journey of healing. While their victories have come at a great price, all will tell you that it was worth everything they invested and more. In my own journey of recovery from trauma, I want to learn from the voice of experience. Spouses are trauma survivors. We are survivors of devastating trauma. Some days we survive better than others. Let's reflect on the voice of experience in this journey. Consider what people like Debbie and Melissa can teach us about taking the journey of a spouse. As you reflect on their stories, are there things that you can identify with? Have you found yourself trying to make it on your own, only to wind up frustrated? Alcoholics Anonymous has an old saying that goes, "your best thinking is what got you where you are." When we find ourselves beating our heads against a wall it's time to listen to people who have experienced this road and are willing to share the lessons learned.

Think about the themes that come through the stories of Melissa, Debbie, and the others who shared their journeys in this book. They provide pearls of wisdom for the journey. They paint a picture of what this journey can be.

Pearls Of Wisdom

Don't blame yourself for the addict's problem. You didn't cause it, you can't control it, and you can't cure it. Put the mental measuring stick in the trash can. Comparing yourself to pictures and people won't heal your wounds.

Don't minimize the grief and pain. Take what you are going through seriously and seek all of the help you need. Don't try and pretend that it doesn't hurt when it's one of the most agonizing things you will experience in your life.

Face your own trauma. You have wounds that need to heal, many of which were there before you married a sex addict. These traumas will continue to cry out for healing if they are ignored. Take them seriously.

Extend trust slowly. Allow yourself to test the waters. Wade in without diving headfirst into deep water. Let the addict court you again. Let him/her earn your respect by presenting themselves as trustworthy. Make decisions about how much to trust and when to do it. Take responsibility for your decisions to trust. Don't see trust as "all or nothing."

Stay in community. You will need your sisters on this journey. If you are a male spouse you will need other men. Recovery requires a group: a team of people who will provide support, hope, honesty, and truth.

Don't make a decision on the relationship for at least one year. Take time to heal. Consider what led you into a marriage with an addict. If you make a fast decision without looking at your own issues, you will probably regret whatever decision is made. Learn all that you can about yourself during this critical time of healing.

Acknowledge your powerlessness and surrender control over the disease. You aren't the cause of the addict's problem and you can't control his/her journey. Surrender control over the uncontrollable.

Identify your coping skills. Look at the healthy ways you cope with stress and pressure. Identify the unhealthy ones. Go through a period of abstinence from your primary coping skill. It's possible that the way you cope may have become an idol.

Be honest about your emotions, even with God. God already knows what you're feeling. Go ahead and say it out loud. Your emotions are created by God and you need to be honest with them. Don't say things are ok when they aren't. Emotional truth is as important as facts.

Give up the martyr/savior complex. It's hard to give up rescue fantasies. They feel so noble. However, the end result is more pain for you as a spouse. The energy that goes into saving someone while destroying yourself is exhausting.

Destroy the emotional measuring tape. Don't compare yourself to airbrushed images, models, and prostitutes. You're too good for that. The addiction is not about you. You are enough. The addiction existed before you were ever introduced to him or her.

Retire the private eye badge. There is no relief in search and seizure; only misery. Intimacy can't be built through spying. The time, techniques, and energy that go into checking phone records, credit card statements, brief cases, and the like will ultimately drain you. No amount of detective work will keep you from feeling vulnerable.

Self-care is critical. The first six months of this journey will be exhausting. The meetings, phone calls, reading, therapy, support groups, and workshops will wear you out. Try to get good sleep, eat right, and take care of yourself.

Your recovery is important. Make it a top priority. Yes, the addict in your life must be in recovery as well. This doesn't mean that yours is less important. We now know that when a spouse enters recovery, the chances of the addict succeeding in attaining sobriety go up significantly. You are worth it. You have been wounded and need healing. Make your meetings, phone calls, and therapy non-negotiable.

Closing Thoughts

As we place this book in your hands, we do so with the hope that it will do more than help you survive. Spouses of sexual addicts can thrive. The wounds can heal. Marriages can thrive with renewed intimate connections. Listen to the words of experience. Think carefully about the stories you have read in this book. Men and women who take this journey are some of the most inspiring people I have ever known. Their stories are challenging and inspirational.

"A bold, loving woman is a warrior who is willing to risk and fight for an intimate relationship with the one she loves. She moves toward her husband, going to battle at her husband's side.[48] She refuses to remain a co-addict and does not enable her husband to comfortably continue being a sexual addict. She does not allow him to abuse her, and takes her own safety physically, emotionally, and spiritually as seriously as she does his. She does not retreat in pain, cowering in fear and hiding in half-truths and illusions. She does not attempt to control her husband, but instead sets and keeps healthy boundaries for herself. She forgives as Christ forgives, loves as God loves, and is always aware of her own need for mercy. Her dependence on God's mercy and strength in her brokenness allows her to step into the future with hope, ever rejoicing in the Lord's bounty toward her. Such a woman drives back the darkness of the evil one and brings in the kingdom of God. She is truly beautiful; the Light shines brightly; the angels sing; Adam cries out; she is Woman."[49]

May God give you a clear vision filled with hope and strength as you experience your personal journey of healing.

Appendix A

WORDS TO AID YOU

Developing an Emotional Vocabulary

LOVE, CONCERN

Admired	Adorable	Accepted	Affectionate
Agreeable	Appreciated	Benevolent	Benign
Brotherly	Caring	Charitable	Comforting
Compassionate	Content	Congenial	Conscientious
Considerate	Cordial	Courteous	Dedicated
Devoted	Empathetic	Fair	Faithful
Forgiving	Friendly	Generous	Genuine
Giving	Good	Helpful	Honest
Honorable	Hospitable	Humane	Interested
Just	Kind	Kindly	Lenient
Lovable	Loving	Mellow	Mild
Confident	Neighborly	Nice	Obliging
Open	Optimistic	Patient	Peaceful

Pleasant	Polite	Reasonable	Receptive
Reliable	Respectful	Relaxed	Responsible
Sensitive	Sympathetic	Sweet	Tender
Thoughtful	Tolerant	Truthful	Trustworthy
Understanding	Unselfish	Warm	Whole
Wonderful			

JOY, GLAD

Alive	Blissful	Brilliant	Calm
Cheerful	Comical	Contented	Delighted
Ecstatic	Elated	Elevated	Enchanted
Enthusiastic	Exalted	Excellent	Excited
Fantastic	Fit	Gay	Glad
Glorious	Good	Grand	Gratified
Great	Happy	Humorous	Inspired
Jovial	Joyful	Jubilant	Magnificent
Majestic	Marvelous	Pleased	Pleasant
Proud	Satisfied	Splendid	Superb
Terrific	Thrilled	Tremendous	Triumphant
Vivacious	Wonderful	Vital	

COMPETENT

Able	Adequate	Assured	Authoritative
Bold	Brave	Capable	Confident
Courageous	Determined	Durable	Dynamic
Effective	Energetic	Fearless	Firm

Forceful	Gallant	Hardy	Healthy
Heroic	Important	Influential	Intense
Manly	Mighty	Powerful	Robust
Secure	Sharp	Skillful	Spirited
Stable	Stouthearted	Strong	Sure
Tough	Virile		

DEPRESSION, SADNESS

Abandoned	Agitated	Alien	Alienated
Alone	Awful	Battered	Blue
Burned	Cheapened	Crushed	Debased
Defeated	Despair	Estranged	Excluded
Exhausted	Forlorn	Forsaken	Fragile
Gloomy	Glum	Grim	Guilt
Hopeless	Horrible	Humiliated	Hurt
Jilted	Kaput	Lonely	Lousy
Low	Miserable	Mistreated	Moody
Mournful	Ostracized	Pathetic	Pitiful
Rebuke	Regretful	Rejected	Reprimanded
Rotten	Ruined	Run down	Stranded
Tearful	Terrible	Unhappy	Unloved
Whipped	Worthless	Wrecked	Wounded
victimized			

ANXIETY, FEAR

Afraid	Agitated	Alarmed	Anxious
Apprehensive	Bashful	Concerned	Desperate
Dreadful	Embarrassed	Fearful	Fidgety
Frantic	`frightened	Hesitant	Horrified
Insecure	Intimidated	Jealous	Jittery
Jumpy	Nervous	On edge	Overwhelmed
Panicky	Perturbed	Restless	Scared
Shaky	Shy	Strained	Tense
Terrified	Threatened	Timid	Uncomfortable
Uneasy	Worrying		

DISTRESS

Afflicted	Alone	Anguish	Awkward
Baffled	Bewildered	Clumsy	Confused
Constrained	Crushed	Defeated	Disgusted
Disliked	Displeased	Dissatisfied	Distrustful
Disturbed	Doubtful	Foolish	Fragile
Futile	Grief	Helpless	Hindered
Hopeless	Impaired	Impatient	Imprisoned
Lost	Nauseated	Offended	Pained
Perplexed	Puzzled	Rejected	Ridiculous
Sickened	Skeptical	Speechless	Strained
Suspicious	Unsatisfied	Unsure	Worried

INADEQUATE

Anemic	Broken	Cowardly	Crippled
Defective	Deficient	Demoralized	Disabled
Exhausted	Exposed	Fragile	Frail
Helpless	Inadequacy	Incapable	Incompetent
Ineffective	Inept	Inferior	Insecure
Meek	Powerless	Puny	Shaken
Sickly	Small	Trivial	Unable
Uncertain	Unfit	Unimportant	Unqualified
Unsound	Useless	Vulnerable	weak

GUILT, SHAME

Ashamed	Abused	Bad	Degraded
Detested	Disgraced	Failure	Humiliated
Ignored	Regretful	Rejected	Unimportant
Ugly	Unloved	Stupid	Tormented
worthless			

ANGER

Agitated	Aggravated	Aggressive	Angry
Annoyed	Arrogant	Belligerent	Biting
Blunt	Bullying	Callous	Combative
Cool	Cranky	Critical	Cross
Cruel	Disagreeable	Disgusted	Displeased
Envious	Fierce	Furious	Hard

Harsh	Hostile	Impatient	Inconsiderate
Indifferent	Irritated	Insensitive	Intolerant
Mad	Mean	Nasty	Obstinate
Provoked	Savage	Severe	Spiteful
Upset	Uptight	Unsound	Useless
Vengeful	Vicious	Vindictive	Violent
Vulnerable	Wrath		

Appendix B

Making the Church a Safe Place: Tips for Church Leaders

Can the church be a safe place for spouses of sex addicts? The church is supposed to be a healing community. The ministry of Jesus focused on healing hurting people. From its beginning, the church has been made up of imperfect human beings who struggle with every sin and compulsive behavior known to mankind. With all of this humanity, how can the church be safe?

No community of people will ever be perfectly safe. Where there are people involved, there will never be a guarantee of complete safety. Relationships are a challenge. Support groups, marriages, families, churches, and any other setting that involves interaction with people, will be difficult. Some groups will be safer than others. There are churches today that are devoting significant resources to meeting the needs of spouses and addicts.

Recently I visited with a group from a church with a strong desire to begin ministering to sex addicts and their families. One of their pastors had just been discovered to have been using Internet pornography. The church's response was to ban him and his wife from any contact with the church. Their decision was made out of ignorance. It wasn't made with a judgmental spirit. Upon educating themselves about sexual addiction, they began to develop a program that would meet the needs of people in their community. They also developed a plan to restore the pastor who had fallen. Apologies were extended for the way that the family had been rejected when they needed to be embraced. Spouses have been harmed by well-meaning church leaders. At times the church may need to repent and make amends with people in recovery. This can make the church a much safer place to be.

I have asked spouses what they were expecting when they went to the church for help. These are some of the things that they have shared: Some spouses report being treated with gentleness and acceptance when they sought help from church leaders. Others didn't get the response they needed. The suggestions in this chapter are the voice of their experience. Our goal is to make the church a safer place for people in recovery.

1. Believe them and affirm their value to the church family

    When a spouse comes to you for help, don't question whether or not she has told you the truth. She is in pain. She has been traumatized. Nobody gets all of the details exactly right when going through a crisis. When a spouse has discovered her husband's extramarital affairs, it doesn't pay to focus on details of the acting out. Whether it has been one affair or many, the pain of betrayal and feeling of rejection is overwhelming. She isn't making up a dramatic story to get your attention. The hurt is real. Don't say, "It's just your imagination" or "it isn't really that bad, is it?" These statements are minimizing and shaming. The spouse has experienced enough shame and humiliation prior to coming into your office. Don't create more for her. Let her know that the church is made up of hurting people and that you want to do your part in helping her feel like she is a part of the church family. She is valuable no matter what problems she is experiencing. She may need to take a break from areas of service to allow time to work on her situation. Let her know that it's ok and that she can count on your support.

2. Don't be judgmental

    Pastors and church leaders are in difficult positions due to the expectations that have been placed on them by church members, or perhaps themselves. There is the perception, and often the expectation, that the pastor should be able to address every situation that the church member confronts. It's important to remember that your pastor is trained to be a pastor, not a counselor. He isn't trained as a specialist in sexual addiction or most other problems. When we feel pressure to produce answers and we don't feel prepared, we retreat into what we know best. This may not always be appropriate for a spouse who is coming in a state of crisis.

For example, if the pastor feels pressure to produce a specific plan for the spouse but doesn't know how, he may retreat into quoting scriptures. The theology may be accurate, but the timing is off. Odds are quoting scriptures about submission and winning over an unbelieving husband, will not address the needs of a spouse in crisis. If she hears things like "are you submitting?" "how's your prayer life?," "have you been consistent with your quiet times?," it will make her question her own faith instead of focusing on solving the problem. It will also make her question her own reality which is what the addict will have been trying to do to her all along. This will make her feel like the church is aligning with her husband against her and safety will be destroyed. Don't remind her of how messy the house was the last time you visited her home or how she needs to be a better parent. Don't question the quality of her cooking. And definitely don't question whether or not she is having sex "enough" to satisfy her husband. I spoke with a spouse recently who went to a pastor for help with her husband. The pastor shook his finger in the spouse's face and said, "The whole problem here is that you won't submit. If you will do what your husband tells you to do, it will solve this problem." She left completely demoralized, questioning her faith, and feeling hopeless. She now felt that she had been let down by her husband, her family, and God.

The use of scripture and prayer can be a powerful part of recovery. They can also be misused and create harm for a spouse. She knows she hasn't been perfect and doesn't need you to remind her of her faults. There will be a time for her to look at her issues, but this isn't what she needs during the initial crisis of discovery.

3. Think safety

Safety is a basic desire that all human beings crave. This is true physically and emotionally. Many have left the church during times of crisis because it wasn't perceived to be a safe place. The tips in this chapter can help create a safe environment for healing. Confidentiality is essential for safety. She needs to know that the pastor won't be taking her story to the church leadership or include it in his next sermon. If a support group exists, it must be confidential.

Spouses need a place to process emotions and pain. Emotional validation will go a long way towards creating safety. During times of crisis, the level of anger and shock may lead a spouse to make shocking statements. She may even be angry with God. If so, God is big enough to take it. He already knows the truth anyway. Refusing to express these feelings doesn't change the fact that you feel them. Don't judge them or preach a sermon when they use abusive language. Let them know that you understand that their pain is real. Validate their fears, anger, hurt, shock, and any other emotions they may express. Validating emotions doesn't mean that you endorse content. When a spouse expresses her feelings of anger towards the addict, it doesn't mean that you support her harming her husband. Yes, the pain is understandable. It's ok to feel what you feel and think what you think. Feelings are amoral. They aren't right or wrong. They are like electrical currents that run through your body. Choosing to act on them will get into the category of right and wrong, legal and illegal. Allow for a long period of grieving. Expect spouses to ride an emotional roller coaster. Grieving is not a linear process. There are many ups and downs. It will feel like "one step forward and two steps back" for awhile. Do what it takes to create a place of emotional safety.

4. If you don't know how to help, say so.

If you aren't familiar with how to provide a treatment plan for the spouse and the addict, that's ok. As a pastor you are trained to be a pastor. You aren't trained to be a counselor and you don't have to have all of the answers. You can validate emotions and create a place of safety. You can be a valuable support resource for spouses and addicts. There are things as a pastor that you will be able to do that a counselor can't. You can provide spiritual support and model the concept of grace: a teaching many spouses and addicts have never known. Tell the spouse that you can understand the pain, validate the feelings, and that they won't have to walk alone. Reassure her that she will have pastoral support along the way. Tell her that you will find her help and that that you will work with her to secure the best possible resources for her situation. You will be amazed at the positive impact you can have on a spouse's recovery.

5. Know your limitations

Pastors may feel pressure from church members or from within themselves to do things they aren't able to do. As a church leader, you don't have to be everything to everyone. Work to establish a referral list in your community of competent counselors who can provide professional therapy. Build relationships with people who can provide counseling and other forms of support. Know who specializes in individual counseling, addiction counseling, marriage & family counseling, and working with children. Keep a list of group resources such as L.I.F.E. groups, 12-step groups, and any other support groups in your area.

Practical resources may be needed. Some spouses need childcare so that they can go to counseling and attend groups. Transportation, housing, and other resources may be needed. Recovery is expensive and there may be financial needs. Even with the cost of treatment, recovery never costs as much as addiction.

Don't put yourself down or minimize your own contribution to making the church a safe place for spouses and addicts. Educating the church on the issues of sexual addiction and its impact both in the church and in families, will be a significant part of your role. Recently, I worked with a couple who allowed their pastor to attend several of their counseling sessions. This church leader has now gained a greater understanding of the impact of sexual addiction. He's now providing support for several couples and educating his church on how they can help people struggling with sexual addiction. The impact of his ministry will be felt for years to come.

6. Walk with people in pain without trying to fix them

This is a challenge. It's hard to walk with someone in pain knowing that you may have some answers but that the spouse may not be in a place to hear them. Go through the period of grief and mourning with the spouse first, then work on plans for the journey. When spouses are hurting, they need someone to walk alongside as they face feelings and situations they never imagined, not try to fix them. Think about the story of Job. This was a man who was stricken with grief and pain that most people couldn't imagine in their worst nightmares. Physical injuries, the loss of his family, and abandonment of friends, were just some of the calamities Job experienced. Notice how his friends responded. Job 2:13 says "Then they sat on the ground with him for seven days and seven nights. No one said a word to him, because they saw how great his suffering was." Your role as a pastor may be to make yourself available and walk through the pain with a spouse. Job's friends did well until they began talking. Advice-giving and evaluations don't work. Later Job says, "A despairing man should have the devotion of his friends, even though he forsakes the fear of the almighty." (Job 6:14). He laments how undependable his brothers are, by saying that they are as "undependable as intermittent streams." (Job 6:15). As a pastor, listen patiently, validate emotions, and be available. The impact you will have on a hurting spouse will be amazing.

7. Don't take sides

This is an easy trap to fall into when you only hear one side of the story. It may be that you don't have access to the addict. You may not have a relationship with the addict when the spouse comes to you for help. This may be a good time to form one. It can be hard not to get caught up in the complex nature of the story. Remember that spouses and addicts both need help. Both need a safe place to heal. They will need a safe community as a couple. Some couples have a time of separation during the healing process. The church can help both parties with living arrangements. Taking sides and creating alliances against either the addict or the spouse, may keep them focused on the other person. This can prevent them from experiencing the individual healing that they need. Listen to the spouse and the addict, provide resources for them, and be an encouragement to them on their journey of recovery.

8. Educate yourself and the church

Church leaders need to learn all that they can about sexual addiction. Sexual addiction is the Christian's drug of choice. Sex addicts aren't perverts wearing trench coats. Don't think that your church is exempt. Western culture is saturated with sex. This is a problem that is only going to get worse. Digital technology, phone lines, wireless capability, and the Internet are all improving. Studies show that 40% of Internet traffic is viewing adult web sites. Viewing sexual stimuli is the number one sexual activity in the United States. Christians aren't immune to this epidemic.

Resources are available that can be used to educate the church on the impact of sexual addiction. A list of books is available in the resources section of this book. The authors of this book conduct seminars in churches designed to educate and equip the church to meet the needs of addicts and spouses. L.I.F.E. Ministries International provides resources for churches to start support groups for male & female addicts, spouses, and young men. A powerful way to educate the church is to have addicts and spouses share their stories. Teach people about the impact of the Internet and its role in making pornography and chat rooms more accessible.

Provide resources for sex education. Silence is addiction's best friend. In a survey of over 100 male addicts, the most common form of sexual trauma listed was the failure of the church and family to provide sex education. Train youth workers and Sunday school teachers to work with families in providing sex education. Educating children about sex is not an option. Who will provide this education? If the church and families don't, the pornography industry will. Begin teaching that sex is created by God and it is a positive, exciting, dynamic part of the marriage relationship. Remove messages of guilt and shame from references to sexuality. This fuels the cycle of addiction.

Avoid sending shaming messages to spouses and family members of addicts. Provide hope and support for them. Let them know that they are a valuable part of the church family. Give them the acceptance that they need. Give them a safe place to heal.

9. Be hopeful!

The impact of sexual addiction can have a positive outcome. Relationships of people in recovery are often deeper and more intimate than people could ever imagine. People are successful when they do the work of recovery. The level of honesty that people in recovery attain can take a marriage beyond where it has ever been.

Provide messages of hope and support for the spouse. Let her know that no matter what happens with the addict, she is a valuable part of the church family. She has gifts that need to be used after experiencing her own healing. Let her know how valuable she is for who she is, not for what she does. Many spouses have become accustomed to performance based acceptance. They may have received many accolades for their work. Let them know that they have hope and that they are special because of who they are.

10. Begin a ministry to spouses and addicts in your community

After a spouse goes through her own healing, she may desire to start support groups or some form of outreach to others in the church and community, experiencing the painful impact of sexual addiction. As the church becomes aware of the problem and creates a safe environment, addicts and spouses will begin to be a part of the church family.

Start a L.I.F.E. group. Make your facility available for 12-step meetings. Consider programs like Celebrate Recovery. Use combinations of all of the above. Encourage people to become mentors to people in recovery. You will be amazed at how addicts and spouses can transform the church in a positive way.

Churches that have committed themselves to becoming safe places for addicts and spouses experience unprecedented growth. Safety, acceptance, and connection are basic desires of all people. Healing takes place in community. As the church commits itself to providing a nurturing setting, healing and transformation will inevitably take place.

Conclusion

The church was intended to be a place of love, acceptance, community, healing, and transformation. Maturing in faith may challenge some boundaries and traditions. I remember watching a church go through a five year transition. Things began when a treatment program in their community asked them to begin providing Bible studies and recovery activities. Over time, more treatment centers began participating. Addicts and their family members began to be mentored in lifeskills and recovery. Over 300 addicts and their families now consider this church their home. For many, their relationship with their mentor has filled the void left by trauma and abandonment. Many have reached the 12th step or the 7th L.I.F.E.

principle and are now bringing others into what they have found to be a safe and healing community.

The most dramatic transformation hasn't been in the addicts and spouses. It has been in the people who were willing to move outside of their comfort zones and begin touching the lives of hurting people. This church will never be the same because they chose to create a home for people who needed safe community.

As a pastor, minister, or church leader, you can lead the way into an era of transformation beyond what you have imagined. It will be a rocky road at times, but seeing changed lives will be worth the effort. The role you can play in the recovery of spouses and addicts is invaluable. It will seem like a thankless job at times, as you watch people you pour your life into fail. However, others will make changes that will motivate and inspire your heart.

Appendix C

Stolen Innocence:
Sexual Addiction and Children

Image is a powerful thing. Image has the ability to control, manipulate, and destroy. It has the power to rob one of innocence. The images we allow our eyes to see courtesy of the Internet, movies, or a magazine are one example. Accidental or not, the exposure a child might have to sexually explicit images can be most destructive. Our children are the most vulnerable.

The impact of sexual addiction on children of sex addicts needs special attention. As the spouse is impacted by sexual acting out, so are the children of the addict. The child can be involved in acting out, or they may develop codependent behaviors. Children may choose to cope by isolating as "lost children." They may become a perfectionist, believing if they would behave better the problem might disappear. They may become "scapegoats" who become oppositional, rebellious, and self-destructive in an attempt to have their needs fulfilled.

The portrait of the child of a sex addict is as different as the individual. I was interviewed several years ago by People magazine for an article entitled "The Cyberporn Generation." The article gives an overview of how pornography is affecting children. The role the child assumes in the family can affect the response as well. Seventeen year old Tyler, was given the responsibility of keeping codes to the filtering system on the family computer. His father had a sexual addiction. Tyler was placed in charge but in the process became addicted to pornography as well. A teenager can't be responsible for his father's recovery.

Eleven year old Sam, decided the videos his father was viewing were destroying the family. Sam began spying on dad, discovering his hiding places so he could dispose of the videos when his father was unaware. He began "policing" his parents in an effort to improve the environment. Once again, not a fair position in which to place a young person.

Finally, there is the example of fourteen year old Cynthia. This young girl decided it was her job to help mom overcome her addictions to smoking and extra-marital affairs. While her father had custody of her, Cynthia felt she could "save" her mom from her addictive behaviors if she would move back into the home. She thought she could hide mom's cigarettes, and mom would decide to not allow men spend the night if her daughter was there. Cynthia began to work on "rescue fantasies."

As teens, children of sex addicts may move toward destructive relationships themselves. Sixteen year old Laurie began dating men who would physically and emotionally abuse her. Regardless of how severe the beatings, she remained in the relationship. The abuser would promise to "never hurt her again" and she would choose to return for more pain. Children may learn to bond with the people who hurt them, thus leading to a pattern of destructive relationships.

As stated earlier, children of sex-addicts are most vulnerable. The children may learn to connect with people who hurt them. A call was received from a pastor of a church concerning a seven year old boy who was acting out sexually during vacation Bible school. The child was in the custody of a man who identifies himself as having an unwanted same sex attraction. The young boy had been viewing the man's DVD collection of pornography-- mostly same sex. The young boy acted out sexually with the little girls in the neighborhood as well as at church. He learned from his "guardian" that this was what boys are supposed to do. The ten year old sister is functioning as the man's caretaker-- balancing the checkbook, paying bills, and providing care to the HIV positive man who is ill. She hides the porn collection when she finds it, but stays very focused trying to function as an adult at age ten! She is growing up way too soon.

More than the loss of innocence

Yes, children of sex-addicts can experience a loss of innocence, impacting them for a lifetime without proper intervention. But there are other losses as well. With loss comes the experience of grieving. A case example involves a female addict who was having multiple affairs with men living in her neighborhood. At one point in her journey Cecilia had affairs going with 5 different men who lived on her street. Her children were playmates of the affair partners' children. As a part of her recovery the children were no longer able to see their friends. It was the loss of friendships for the children which caused tremendous grief.

In addition to the loss of relationships, children may experience the loss of social activities. Money may not be readily available because of the cost of recovery programs or counseling, or because of a job loss due to the addict's acting out. Participation in gymnastics or baseball may seem insignificant in comparison to recovery, but it represents some semblance of normality for the child. The children may have to move, changing school districts in the process. They would need to cope with both the change in environment and relationships. This is difficult for any child, but for a child living with a sex-addict it is one more loss to grieve.

The image of a parent falling off a pedestal is another loss for the child to grieve. While the child may not be able to articulate it, respect is lost and trust is broken. In the child's mind, a healthy model of marriage and intimacy is destroyed, at least temporarily. The child may react with fear and anxiety. In the process of recovery it is important that fear and anxiety be replaced with hope and security.

Serious consequences

As stated earlier, image is powerful. Intentionally or accidentally, children of sex-addicts are often exposed to pornography. The child may be exposed to sexually explicit material long before they are developmentally ready to cope. Pornography coming into the home on a computer can be accessed easily by a child. Children are Internet savvy. Once porn is discovered on a home computer, it is important to ask the child if they have seen any of these images.

Children who see pornography (accidentally) often feel dirty and experience intense shame reactions. Use caution in addressing this shame. It is essential you reassure the child they have done nothing wrong. Help the child to understand we all have to guard our hearts since this type of material is saturating our culture. Use the opportunity to discuss with them the difference between addictive and unhealthy sexuality and God's healthy design for sexuality.

Early imprinting of pornography on the child's brain can have serious consequences if not addressed as quickly as possible. The images stay with the child and they must learn to manage these intrusive thoughts. In some cases, children can get hooked on porn due to exposure at an early age. If this occurs, seek professional help for the child. Avoid shaming him/her. Assure the child it is great the problem is being addressed early in life before it becomes a more serious issue.

The Arousal Template

Early sexual arousal forms what sex addiction specialists refer to as the arousal template. Early sexual excitement shapes the brain for later sexual excitement. The impact on neuropathways in the brain is being documented in spect brain imaging. In adult years, the individual may try to recreate the first experience in an attempt to resolve a traumatic experience. This can give birth to a variety of fetishes.[50]

This chapter is not being written to send you into a panic. Sexual addiction brings trauma to the family. It also comes with opportunities to break the cycle. Sex is the language of culture in the United States. Sexual stimuli invade children on a daily basis. When inappropriate material comes into the presence of your child, it creates an opportunity for a discussion of healthy sexuality. One father shared with me about his experience taking his daughter to a father/daughter

Girl Scout dance. Door prizes had been donated by businesses. His daughter had the winning raffle ticket for one of the gifts. Inside the neatly wrapped package was soap, lotions, and a sex toy. Instead of panicking, the father calmly told his daughter what the toy was and used it as an opportunity to discuss healthy sexuality. It's now been almost 7 years since that dance. The daughter is almost 17 and has a wonderful perspective on God's design for sex.

The impact of sexual addiction in your home can't be minimized. It also shouldn't be catastrophized. Like other forms of trauma, this one can be redeemed. Make the most of your opportunities for discussions of healthy sexuality with your children.

To parents of children and adolescent sex-addicts

As the parent of a child addicted to pornography there are steps you can take to reclaim your child's purity. Boundaries of protection must be provided. To the addicted child, the boundaries will seem unnecessary or unreasonable. You must remind yourself it is merely "addict-talk" as they attempt to vocalize their disapproval.

Practically, the parent has the right and responsibility of controlling access to the Internet. Computer (porn) filtering systems must be researched, purchased and installed. The systems must be password protected, with the information available only to the adult non-sex-addict in the household. If the child has access to a computer in their room, it might be wise to have a "no closed door" policy while the computer is in use. Knowing your child's friends well enough to know whether or not those households have proper filtering systems is helpful. Knowing the character of the friend (and the friend's family) the child spends time with is important as well.

Dan shared his first exposure to pornography. His father had a problem with sexual addiction. As a 16 year old, Dan was put in charge of the passwords and monitoring the Internet in his family. By the age of 17, Dan was as addicted as his father. The parent became the child and the child became the parent. Parents must take responsibility for protecting their homes. Even with Internet filters, children will continue to be exposed to sexual images and references on a daily basis. Make a commitment to break the "don't talk" rule discussed in chapter 3.

Professional counseling is essential if the child is to successfully overcome his addiction for the long term. Choosing a counselor who is an expert in the field of sexual addiction will help tremendously as the child moves toward recovery. It may be necessary for other family members to be involved in the recovery process. As is true with adult sex-addicts, often individuals close to the minor sex-addict are affected by the behavior and may need help to cope, heal, and rebuild.

One final thought

As parents, it is not about blaming or shaming ourselves if we have a child who is addicted to pornography, however, it is an opportunity for us to examine our own standards of purity. We can't have a double-standard when it comes to parenting our children. Our example is important as we attempt to model a healthy marriage and good relational intimacy. May the little eyes that are watching, watch only that which is pure and right.

Resource List

<u>**Books**</u>

Healing the Wounds of Sexual Addiction	Mark Laaser
Pure Desire	Ted Roberts
Living With Your Husbands Secret Wars	Marsha Means
Codependent No More	Melodie Beattie
False Intimacy	Harry Schaumburg
Beyond Betrayal	Jennifer Schneider
Out of the Shadows	Patrick Carnes
The Betrayal Bond	Patrick Carnes
Breaking Free	Russell Willingham
Breaking Free	Beth Moore
Wednesday's Child	Suzanne Sommers
Beyond the storm	Jerry Jones
A L.I.F.E. Guide for Spouses	Melissa Haas
Healing the Shame that Binds You	John Bradshaw
Homecoming	John Bradshaw
Boundaries	Henry Cloud & John Townsend
Safe People	Henry Cloud & John Townsend
When God Becomes a Drug	Father Leo Booth
Toxic Faith	Jack Felton/ Steve Arterburn
The Subtle Power of Spiritual Abuse	David Johnson & Jeff VanVonderen

Churches that Abuse   Ronald Enroth
The Art of Forgiveness   Lewis Smedes
Your Sexually Addicted Spouse   Dr. Barbara Steffens
                                       and Marsha Means

Recovery Bible

Journey of Recovery New Testament, International Bible Society, 2006.

Grieving

A Grief Observed   C.S. Lewis
Surprised by Joy   C.S. Lewis
On Death and Dying   Elizabeth Kubler Ross
Recovering From the Losses of Life   H. Norman Wright
Experiencing Grief   H. Norman Wright

Cd's & DVD's

Facing the Fire: Sexual Addiction and the Church - Richard Blankenship

Finding a counselor

American Association of Certified Christian Sexual Addiction Specialists

www.sexaddictioncertification.org. AACCSAS maintains a database of professionals with a specialty in treating sex addicts and their families.

CAPS International

Christian Association for Psychological Studies provides resources for professional Christian counselors. Be aware in using their registry that occasionally some are listed who are pastoral counselors or lay counselors. While this isn't the norm, we encourage you to exercise caution in using this resource. www.caps.net

National Board of Certified Counselors
www.nbcc.org has a database of nationally certified counselors. You will need to ask the counselor if he/she is knowledgeable in the area of sex addiction.

This section also contains suggestions on how to find a counselor and what some questions you might ask.

Workshops

Faithful and True Marriages does intensive therapeutic weekends for couples in recovery. Workshops are held occasionally for spouses in recovery as well. These are typically 3-4 days of intensive therapeutic work. For more information on the couples retreats see the web site at www.faithfulandtruemarriages.org.

Faithful and True Atlanta
Richard Blankenship directs one of the few programs in the Christian community that offers groups and workshops for spouses, male addicts, female addicts, and couples in recovery. For more information visit the web site www.christiansexualintegrity.org.

Dimensional Journey Boot Camp
This is an experiential program led by Cliff and Jeani Poe. It is not specific to sex addiction, though it is beneficial to a wide variety of people. The work done during these workshops helps with overcoming past obstacles and developing a healthier view of forgiveness. www.dimensionaljourney.com

National Organizations
SASH (Society for the Advancement of Sexual Health) secular organization dedicated to providing resources for treating sexual addiction and families of sex addicts. A membership registry provides access to clinicians specializing in treating sexual addicton. www.sash.net.

The National Coalition for the Protection of Children and Families is based in Cincinnati, Ohio. They have many offices around the United States and address the needs of spouses and addicts by educating the public and working at all levels of federal and state government. www.nationalcoalition.org

Support Groups

L.I.F.E. Ministries International is based near Orlando, Florida. They provide resources for churches and support groups around the world. Their workbook series is edited by Dr. Mark Laaser and contains excellent support group material. There is a workbook for spouses by Melissa Haas. These materials are also being translated into foreign languages. To find a L.I.F.E. group or order workbooks go to www.freedomeveryday.org.

For Men Only/For Women Only is part of the work of Ted and Diane Roberts. They provide support groups in churches around the United States for male sex addicts and spouses of sex addicts. http://puredesire.org/what/partner.asp

About the Author

Richard Blankenship has worked with churches and counseling centers for almost 25 years. Richard is involved in many activities related to treating sexual addiction and spouses of sex addicts. He is the cofounder of the American Association of Certified Christian Sexual Addiction Specialists (along with Dr. Mark Laaser). This organization provides certification for professional counselors and church leaders working in the field of sexual addiction. In 2002, Richard began the North Atlanta Center for Christian Counseling and Faithful and True – Atlanta. Today, Faithful and True – Atlanta is one of the few faith-based programs in the United States that offers groups and services for spouses of sex addicts, male addicts, female addicts, and couples in recovery. The North Atlanta Center for Christian Counseling provides professional counseling services for a wide variety of issues. The highly trained professional staff provides individual, marital, and family counseling. Cornerstone Psychotherapy also works with Richard in providing professional counseling services.

In addition, Richard founded Cornerstone Training, an organization dedicated to providing quality continuing education programs for counselors and church leaders. Many of these programs provide education and supervision opportunities for those seeking certification with the American Association of Certified Christian Sexual Addiction Specialists. They are an approved provider for the National Board of Certified Counselors (NBCC).

Faithful and True Marriages brings together therapists who specialize in working with sex addicts and spouses. Under Richard's direction, this organization provides retreats for couples in recovery from sexual addiction. Intensive therapy workshops are also offered for spouses of sex addicts, male addicts, and female addicts. Individual intensives for men, women, and couples are available through Marriage Counseling America.

Contact Information

Faithful and True Marriages	www.faithfulandtruemarriages.org
Faithful and True Atlanta	www.christiansexualintegrity.org
North Atlanta Center for Christian Counseling	www.northatlantachristian.org
Cornerstone Psychotherapy	www.cornerstonepsychotherapy.com
Marriage Counseling America	www.marriagecounselingamerica.org
Cornerstone Training	www.cornerstonetraining.org
Atlanta Stepfamilies	www.StepfamiliesAtlanta.com
About S.A.R.A.H.	www.sarahbook.com
American Association of Certified Christian Sexual Addiction Specialists, Inc.	www.sexaddictioncertification.org

For conferences, workshops, and speaking engagements Richard can be contacted at the location listed below:

Richard Blankenship
2312 Peachford Rd. Suite C
Atlanta, GA 30338
770-457-3028
NACounsel@gmail.com

Acknowledgments and Dedication

Never in my wildest dreams did I believe I would be writing a book. When Johna Hale came and talked with me about writing the L.I.F.E. Guide for Young Men, I said yes, and then went immediately into a panic. I had never written before and had always said I would never write a book. The writing bug bit and I haven't been the same since. Since beginning to work in this field, working with spouses of sex addicts has become a passion. So many of the men and women who have come through our spouses groups have asked for material that would help them focus on the journey of a spouse. I made a difficult decision early in the writing of S.A.R.A.H. I have wanted to share the parts of my trauma story outside of the privacy of a therapist's office. It's been through working with some of this pain that I have connected with so many spouses through the years. Many of the things in chapter 3 have never been shared publicly. I've discovered that sharing stories of healing can bring hope into people's lives. I'm grateful I can share it with you as readers and pray that it will help you in some way.

This book has been written during many late nights and with lots of help. My wife, Vickie, and my daughters Cathy and Emily have tolerated my writing time very graciously. It's been an honor to have so many people in recovery share a part in the lives of our children. Cathy and Emily are growing up with skills and experiences because of these people that they would never have otherwise. They'll always be daddy's little girls. I honor Vickie, Cathy & Emily with this work.

Mark Laaser has supported me through many difficult times. The opportunities he has given me have blessed me immeasurably. It's an honor to call him a teacher and mentor. It's more of an honor to call him a friend. Mark initially led the way for the Christian community to address sexual addiction. God raised him up for this mission and he has been faithful to his calling. He is a shining example of how God heals brokenness and redeems pain.

As trauma survivors, we look for stability. Two people who have always been there have been Dr. Charles (Chuck) Williams and David Blackwell. I can't think of any two counselors that I respect more than these men. David was with me in the early days when I was starting my career. Chuck was a supervisor and director during a very difficult time many years ago. His encouragement and professional example are things I have been able to rely on through the years. Much of his thinking shaped the development of my current practice.

In this edition I included more of my own story. Talking with people from my past has been extremely helpful in understanding my own story. Part of this book was written in the home of Sam and Maureen Ottenlips. Talking with Maureen about the city and church in which we both grew up has helped fill in some gaps and deepen my understanding. I'm grateful for Maureen and her family and the joy they have brought to me. We have a longtime bond that I will always treasure.

Stacey Nyman, Amy Barrett and Dr. Michael Lyles are professionals who have provided care and stability for our family as we have worked through many of the issues you read about in this book. They demonstrate the character, integrity, and compassion and have touched the lives of many people in recovery.

People like Jennifer Schneider, Deborah Corley, Stephanie Carnes, and Barbara Steffens have pioneered in the field of spouse's recovery. Their research and work is invaluable in the area of spouses and recovery. I have tremendous respect and admiration for their work.

Debbie Whitcomb has faced incredible odds over the last several years. Working with her during training events has been inspirational. She has taken the step of being vulnerable with her story in a very public way. Many spouses are taking their journey of recovery because of her work. Debbie is a great friend and coworker.

Mark Richardson and Joyce Tomblin have been with the Faithful and True Atlanta staff since the early days. Mark has faithfully led men's groups, sometimes as many as six a week, for almost seven years. He was vulnerable enough to publish his story of recovery from sexual addiction in the *Atlanta Journal and Constitution*. Many men have had their lives touched by Mark. Joyce has led our spouses groups and has been instrumental in developing this book. Her ideas have helped shape the therapy groups for spouses of sex addicts. I love it when we have male spouses in our groups because it allows me to work with Joyce as a co-leader. She is one of my heroes in this field and her heart for spouses shows.

The staff of the North Atlanta Center for Christian Counseling has grown tremendously. People like Sonya Kennedy, Mindy Pierce, Abbey Foard, Jade Mazarin, Andrea Bartley, Rachel Holcomb, Eric Hoyme, Chuck Anderson, Kathryn Hawkins, Amber Cleveland, Eryn Jones, and Brooks Lines have built this ministry. Brooks contributed several of the ideas that helped begin the writing of this book. Never in my wildest dreams did I believe it would evolve into what it is today. God is doing amazing things!

Several friends and colleagues were gracious enough to review this material. Doug Rosenau and Debra Taylor are published authors and leaders in the field of Christian sex therapy. Doug and his assistant, David Hall, wrote most of the introduction to this book. The acronym of S.A.R.A.H. (Spouses of Addicts Rebuilding and Healing) was Doug's idea. Sharon Borntrager is a great friend and supporter. Sharon began the national help line for the National Coalition for the Protection of Children and Families. Dave Brown continues this work today. This organization, under the leadership of Rick Schatz, does much great work in providing resources for the public which address many of the issues discussed in this book. Rick and Vicki Kardos are wonderful friends and supporters. The Nathan Project was their creation and they do tremendous work in New England. Dr. Barbara Steffens has published research on spouses and trauma. She is a leader in this industry and has a passion for working with spouses. Her work is known nationally. Barbara has one of the most brilliant minds of anyone in the field of sexual addiction and spouses recovery. This book couldn't have been written without her help. Melissa Haas has authored the L.I.F.E. guide for spouses and has influenced much of my thinking. Melissa has helped and inspired many spouses and has shaped much of my thinking. Her influence in this book can't be allowed to go unacknowledged.

Jade Mazarin has been my personal assistant, office manager, and was an editor of the first publication of S.A.R.A.H. She is an author and speaker and likes working with women who have issues with unhealthy attachment in relationships. Her first book entitled *"A Hearts Journey Towards Freedom"* is now available. The revisions to S.A.R.A.H. (*Spouses of Sex Addicts*) would not have been possible without the gifted writing of Sherry Hubright. Sherry has been fantastic to work with on this project. Tina Hock has edited the final manuscript. I'm grateful for her sharp eye and her ability to catch mistakes. Morseo, I'm grateful for her example and her ability to speak the truth in love.

The people I am most grateful for are the thousands of spouses who have attended our groups, counseling sessions, workshops, seminars, and retreats through the years. Many of you shared your stories and ideas with me for inclusion in this book. This book is for you. Without your courage, example, and willingness to take a difficult journey, none of this would've happened. You are the most amazing people I've ever known. I thank God for each of you and what you have taught me through the years.

Dedication
Of the original publication of S.A.R.A.H.

Through the months of writing S.A.R.A.H., there was one name that kept coming to mind. As I would finish a section, I kept thinking, "WWDT– what would Debbie think?" *Debbie Laaser* has been the single greatest influence in the way that we work with spouses at Faithful and True Atlanta. For several years, she has been a constant encouragement to me. Debbie has been a teacher and advisor for the development of our spouses groups. She has been one of my greatest teachers.

Debbie is one of the most naturally gifted therapists I have ever known. Her training came from the school of experience. Debbie has touched the lives of thousands of people in her ministry to spouses of sexual addicts. Her compassion on people is remarkable. She is an inspiration to the people who know her.

In a time where values of loyalty and trust have been abandoned by many, Debbie shines as an example of character, integrity, and trustworthiness. She has a love for people, a heart for ministry, and possesses warmth that draws people to her. Her work with spouses is pioneering in a field where we desperately need great leaders and resources. The work that she does with Mark at Faithful and True Ministries has touched many lives. The influence that she has had on me personally and professionally has been so powerful that there is no way this book could have been written without honoring her for who she is and what she has done in ministry to spouses of sex addicts.

[1] **Introduction**
Journey of Recovery New Testament, International Bible Society, 2006.

Chapter 1

[2] Steffens, Barbara and Means, Marsha. *Your Sexually Addicted Spouse*, New Horizon Publishing, 2009.

[3] Haas, Melissa. *L.I.F.E. Guide for Spouses*. Color House Graphics 2005.

[4] Melissa gives excellent guidelines in the L.I.F.E. guide for spouses on finding and developing safe relationships (p. 27).

[5] *L.I.F.E. Guide for Spouses*. pp. 37-44.

[6] *L.I.F.E. Guide for Spouses* p. 47.

[7] A Grief Observed, C.S. Lewis, p. 65-66. Surprised by Joy is also an excellent book for someone grieving deeply and questioning their faith.

[8] *L.I.F.E. Guide for Spouses* p. 47-48.

[9] *L.I.F.E. Guide for Spouses* p. 48.

[10] Bell, Rob. *Velvet Elvis: Repainting the Christian faith*. Zondervan 2005.

[11] Martin, Terry L. and Doka, Kenneth J., *Men Don't Cry...Women Do: Transcending Gender Stereotypes of Grief*. Routledge, 2000.

[12] The Hiding Place. World Wide Pictures original release 1977, VHS release 2003.

[13] Fowler, W.R. and Greenstone, J.L. *Crisis intervention compendium*. Copley Publishing, 1987.

Chapter 2

[14]   Rhonda's story was shared by a client who had a desire to communicate the depth of hurt and pain experienced in betrayal. Her name was changed to protect her identity.

Chapter 3

[15]   Andreason, Nancy C. "Posttraumatic Stress Disorder," in *Comprehensive Textbook of Psychiatry*, ed. H.I. Kaplan and B.J. Sadock, 4th ed. (Baltimore: Williams and Wilkins, 1985, 918-924.

[16]   http://www.cavalcadeproductions.com/childhood-trauma.html

[17]   Steffens, Barbara. *The Journey of a Spouse*. Lecture at "Sexual Addiction: The Christian's Drug of Choice" conference in Cincinnati, OH. November 4, 2005.

[18]   More information on the research of Dr. Carnes can be found in his book *Don't Call It Love*.

[19]   Langberg, Diane. *Counseling Survivors of Sexual Abuse*. Wheaton, IL: Tyndale House Publishers, Inc. 1997.

[20]   Booth, L. *When God Becomes a Drug*. Tarcher, 1991.

[21]   Bloomfield, H. *Making Peace With Your Parents*. Random House, Inc. 1983.

[22]   Yancey, P. *The Jesus I Never Knew*. Grand Rapids, Michigan. Zondervan Publishing House, 1995.

Chapter 4

[23]   The acronym for "Shame" comes from the work of Cliff & Jeani Poe. Cliff & Jeani run an experiential program in Houston, Texas called "Dimensional Journey."

[24]   Big book of Alcoholics Anonymous (AA) and The Twelve Steps and Twelve Traditions contain the history of twelve-step recovery and information that is valuable no matter what program of recovery you are using. These books can be purchased through most online book stores.

[25]   Ellis, Albert & Robert A. Harper. *A New Guide To Rational Living*. New York: Prentice Hall Publishing, 1975.

[26]   For more information on the Carnes-Delmonico trauma index see Carnes, Patrick. *The Betrayal Bond..* Deer Beach, Florida: Health Communications, 1998.

[27]   Carnes, Patrick. *Out of the shadows*. Minneapolis: Compcare Publishers, 2[nd ed.] 1992.

[28]   Frankl, Victor E. *Man's Search for Meaning: An Introduction to Logotherapy*. New York: Washington Square Press, 1963. The books was also published under the title *From Death-Camp to Existentialism* in 1959. The original publication in German was in 1946.

[29]   The concept of family rules and roles is based on the work of Virginia Satir.

30 Cloud, Henry & John Townsend. *Safe People*. Grand Rapids: Zondervan, 1996. This book contains a further discussion of the qualities of safe people.

31 Nichols, Michael P. & Richard C. Schwartz. *Family Therapy: Concepts and Method (6ᵗʰ edition)s*. Boston: Allyn & Bacon, 2004.

Chapter 5

32 Bugliosi, Vincent and Curt Gentry. *Helter Skelter: The true story of the manson murders*. New York, New York: Norton, 1974

33 Booth, Leo. *When God Becomes A Drug*. Penguin Group Publishers, 1992.

34 Horton, A. L., Wilkins, M. M., & Wright, W. (1988). Women who ended abuse: What religious leaders and religion did for these victims. In A. L. Horton, & J. A. Williamson (Eds.), <u>Abuse and religion: When praying isn't enough</u> (pp. 235-246). Lexington, MA: Lexington

35 Anderson, Bernhard W. *Out of the Depths*. Philadelphia: The Westminster Press, 1983. Brueggemann, Walter. *The Message of the Psalms*. Minneapolis, MN: Augsburg Publishing House, 1984.

36 *Pioneers of Hospice: Changing the Face of Dying*. Madison Deane Initiative. 2004. Film with interviews with Elizabeth Kubler Ross.

Chapter 6

37 Schneider, J., Irons, R. and Corley, D. *Disclosure of extramarital sexual activities by sexually exploitative professionals and other persons with addictive or compulsive sexual disorders*. Journal of sex education and therapy. 1999, 24 (4); 277-287.

38 www.sa.org lists the twelve steps of sexaholics anonymous.

39 Many sayings like this come from Alcoholics Anonymous literature and tradition.

40 AFA statistic found on the web site www.afa.net. Another excellent source of information is the National Coalition for the Protection of Children and Families. www.nationalcoalition.org.

41 Mark 12: 29-31

42 Dressage and CT magazine. 1994. Article by Dietrich von Hopffgarten. Quoted in Whole Horsemanship: An Integrated Approach to Teaching, Training, and Riding by Dianne Lindig Tobin.

43 Linda Kohanov. *The Tao of Equus*. (Novato, CA: New World Library, 2001).

44 Carnes, Patrick, The Betrayal Bond. (Deerfield Beach, FL: Health Communications inc.)

45 Satir, V., Banmen, J., Gerber, J. and Gomori, M. *Satir Model: Family Therapy and Beyond*. (Science and Behavior Books, 1991).

46 Wright, Norman, TJTA Training Series.

47 Cloud, H. and Townsend, J. *Boundaries*. Zondervan: 1992.

[48] Allender, Dr. Dan & Longman, Dr. Tremper. (1995). *Intimate Allies*. Wheaton, IL: Tyndale House Publishers, Inc.

[49] Anderson, Kim. 2005. *The Beauty of Eve Restored*. Unpublished paper.

Appendice C

[50] Amen, Daniel. *The Brain in Love: 12 Lessons to Enhance Your Love Life*. (Random House: July 2009.)

CPSIA information can be obtained at www.ICGtesting.com
Printed in the USA
BVOW01s0027260816

460018BV00002B/194/P